"I was One and then I became Three"

"Something is added to you unlike to what thou see; something animates thy clay higher than all that is the object of thy senses. Behold, what is it? Thy body remains STILL matter after IT is fled, therefore IT is no part of it; IT is immaterial, therefore IT is accountable for its actions."

"...In truth, GOD caused the Neters to be born, the creation of the cities, establishment of the nomes, the establishment of the Neters in their places of adoration. . . GOD made their likenesses according to their desire. Thereby, the Neters entered into their bodies, the variety of wood, all types of mineral, clay, and all things that grow from these and in which they have taken place, foods, provisions, and all good things... He (Ptah) is Horus."

Ancient Egyptian Proverbs

P.O.Box 570459
Miami, Florida, 33257
(305) 378-6253 Fax: (305) 378-6253

First U.S. edition 1996

Second Edition © 1997 By Reginald Muata Ashby

All rights reserved. No part of this book may be used or reproduced in any manner whatsoever without written permission (address above) except in the case of brief quotations embodied in critical articles and reviews. All inquiries may be addressed to the address above.

The author is available for group lectures and individual counseling. For further information contact the publisher.

Ashby, Muata
The Hidden Properties of Matter 1-884564-07-0

Library of Congress Cataloging in Publication Data

1 Yoga 2 Egyptian Philosophy, 3 Eastern Philosophy, 4 Esoterism, 5 Meditation, 6 Self Help.

Cruzian Mystic Books

Also by Muata Ashby

Egyptian Yoga: The Philosophy of Enlightenment
Initiation Into Egyptian Yoga: The Secrets of Sheti
Egyptian Proverbs: Tempt Tchaas,
Mystical Wisdom Teachings and Meditations
The Egyptian Yoga Exercise Workout Book
Mysticism of Ushet Rekhat: Worship of the Divine Mother

For more listings see the back section.

Sema
Institute of Yoga

Sema (⚶) is an Ancient Egyptian word and symbol meaning *union*. The Sema Institute is dedicated to the propagation of the universal teachings of spiritual evolution which relate to the union of humanity and the union of all things within the universe. It is a non-denominational organization which recognizes the unifying principles in all spiritual and religious systems of evolution throughout the world. Our primary goals are to provide the wisdom of ancient spiritual teachings in books, courses and other forms of communication. Secondly, to provide expert instruction and training in the various yogic disciplines including Ancient Egyptian Philosophy, Christian Gnosticism, Indian Philosophy and modern science. Thirdly, to promote world peace and Universal Love.

A primary focus of our tradition is to identify and acknowledge the yogic principles within all religions and to relate them to each other in order to promote their deeper understanding as well as to show the essential unity of purpose and the unity of all living beings and nature within the whole of existence.

The Institute is open to all who believe in the principles of peace, non-violence and spiritual emancipation regardless of sex, race, or creed.

About the author and editor:
Dr. Muata Abhaya Ashby

About The Author

Reginald Muata Ashby holds a Doctor of Philosophy Degree in Religion, and a Doctor of Divinity Degree in Holistic Healing. He is also a Pastoral Counselor and Teacher of Yoga Philosophy and Discipline. Dr. Ashby is an adjunct faculty member of the American Institute of Holistic Theology and an ordained Minister. Dr. Ashby has studied advanced Jnana, Bhakti and Kundalini Yogas under the guidance of Swami Jyotirmayananda, a world renowned Yoga Master. He has studied the mystical teachings of Ancient Egypt for many years and is the creator of the Egyptian Yoga concept. He is also the founder of the Sema Institute, an organization dedicated to the propagation of the teachings of Yoga and mystical spirituality.

Karen Clarke-Ashby "Vijaya-Asha" is the wife and spiritual partner of Muata. She is an independent researcher, practitioner and teacher of Yoga, a Doctor in the Sciences and a Pastoral Counselor, the editor of Egyptian Proverbs and Egyptian Yoga by Muata. ♀

Sema Institute
P.O. Box 570459, Miami, Fla. 33257 (305) 378-6253, Fax (305) 378-6253
©1996

YOGA
Art
Education
Spiritual Practice

Based on the Book

Egyptian Yoga
The Philosophy of Enlightenment

For a complete listing of titles
send for the free *Egyptian Yoga
Catalog*

Table of Contents

Author's Foreword

Who Were the Ancient Egyptians and What is Yoga Philosophy?

The Ancient Egyptian religion (*Shetaut Neter*), language and symbols provide the first "historical" record of Yoga Philosophy and Religious literature. Egyptian Yoga is what has been commonly referred to by Egyptologists as Egyptian "Religion" or "Mythology", but to think of it as just another set of stories or allegories about a long lost civilization is to completely miss the greatest secret of human existence. Yoga, in all of its forms and disciplines of spiritual development, was practiced in Egypt earlier than anywhere else in history. This unique perspective from the highest philosophical system which developed in Africa over seven thousand years ago provides a new way to look at life, religion, the discipline of psychology and the way to spiritual development leading to spiritual Enlightenment. Egyptian mythology, when understood as a system of

Yoga (union of the individual soul with the Universal Soul or Supreme Consciousness), gives every individual insight into their own divine nature and also a deeper insight into all religions and Yoga systems.

Diodorus Siculus (Greek Historian) writes in the time of Augustus (first century B.C.):

"Now the Ethiopians, as historians relate, were the first of all men and the proofs of this statement, they say, are manifest. For that they did not come into their land as immigrants from abroad but were the natives of it and so justly bear the name of au-tochthones (sprung from the soil itself), *is, they maintain, conceded by practically all men..."*

"They also say that the Egyptians are colonists sent out by the Ethiopians, Osiris having been the leader of the colony. For, speaking generally, what is now Egypt, they maintain, was not

land, but sea, when in the beginning the universe was being formed; afterwards, however, as the Nile during the times of its inundation carried down the mud from Ethiopia, land was gradually built up from the deposit...And the larger parts of the customs of the Egyptians are, they hold, Ethiopian, the colonists still preserving their ancient manners. For instance, the belief that their kings are Gods, the very special attention which they pay to their burials, and many other matters of a similar nature, are Ethiopian practices, while the shapes of their statues and the forms of their letters are Ethiopian; for of the two kinds of writing which the Egyptians have, that which is known as popular (demotic) *is learned by everyone, while that which is called sacred* (hieratic), *is understood only by the priests of the Egyptians, who learnt it from their Fathers as one of the things which are not divulged, but among the Ethiopians, everyone uses these forms of letters. Furthermore, the orders of the priests, they maintain, have much the same position among both peoples; for all are clean who are engaged in the service of the gods, keeping themselves shaven, like the Ethiopian priests, and having the same dress and form of staff, which is shaped like a plough and is carried by their kings who wear high felt hats which end in a knob in the top and are circled by the serpents which they call asps; and this symbol appears to carry the thought that it will be the lot who shall dare to attack the king to encounter death-carrying stings. Many other things are told by them concerning their own antiquity and the colony which they sent out that became the Egyptians, but about this there is no special need of our writing anything."*

The Ancient Egyptian texts state:

> *"Our people originated at the base of the*
> *mountain of the Moon,*
> *at the origin of the Nile river."*

🔺🌙👥

"KMT"
"Egypt", "Burnt", "Land of Black-
ness","Land of the Burnt People." 🔺🌙👥

KMT (Ancient Egypt) is situated close to Lake Victoria in present day Afrika. This is the same location where the earliest human remains have been found, in the land currently known as Ethiopia-Tanzania. Recent genetic technology as reported in the new encyclopedias and leading news publications has revealed that all peoples of the world originated in Afrika and migrated to other parts of the world prior to the last Ice Age 40,000 years ago. Therefore, as of this time, genetic testing has revealed that all humans are alike. The earliest bone fossils which have been found in many parts of the world were those of the African Grimaldi type. During the Ice Age, it was not possible to communicate or to migrate. Those trapped in specific locations were subject to the regional forces of weather and climate. Less warmer climates required less body pigment, thereby producing lighter pigmented people who now differed from their dark-skinned ancestors. After the Ice Age when travel was possible, these light-skinned people who had lived in the northern, colder regions of harsh weather during the Ice Age period moved back to the warmer climates of their ancestors, and mixed with the people there who had remained dark-skinned, thereby producing the Semitic colored people. "Semite" means mixture of skin color shades.

Therefore, there is only one human race who, due to different climactic and regional exposure, changed to a point where there seemed to be different "types"of people. Differences were noted with respect to skin color, hair texture, customs, languages, and with respect to the essential nature (psychological and emotional makeup) due to the experiences each group had to face and overcome in order to survive.

From a philosophical standpoint, the question as to the origin of humanity is redundant when it is understood that *ALL* come from one origin which some choose to call the "Big Bang" and others "The Supreme Being."

> **"Thou makest the color of the skin of one race to be different from that of another, but however many may be the varieties of mankind, it is thou that makes them all to live."**

Ancient Egyptian Proverb from
The Hymns of Amun

> **"Souls, Horus, son, are of the self-same nature, since they came from the same place where the Creator modeled them; nor male nor female are they. Sex is a thing of bodies not of Souls."**

Ancient Egyptian Proverb from *The teachings of Isis to Horus*

Historical evidence proves that Ethiopia-Nubia already had Kingdoms at least 300 years before the first Kingdom-Pharaoh of Egypt.

"Ancient Egypt was a colony of Nubia - Ethiopia. ...Osiris having been the leader of the colony..."

"And upon his return to Greece, they gathered around and asked, "tell us about this great land of the Blacks called Ethiopia." And Herodotus said, "There are two great Ethiopian nations, one in Sind (India) and the other in Egypt."

Recorded by Egyptian high priest *Manetho* (300 B.C.) also Recorded by *Diodorus* (Greek historian 100 B.C.)

The pyramids themselves however, cannot be dated, but indications are that they existed far back in antiquity. The Pyramid Texts (hieroglyphics inscribed on pyramid walls) and Coffin Texts (hieroglyphics inscribed on coffins) speak authoritatively on the constitution of the human spirit, the vital Life Force along the human spinal cord (known in India as *"Kundalini"*), the immortality of the soul, reincarnation and the law of Cause and Effect (known in India as the Law of Karma).

What is Yoga Philosophy and Spiritual Practice

Since a complete treatise on the theory and practice of yoga would require several volumes, only a basic outline will be given here.

When we look out upon the world, we are often baffled by the multiplicity which constitutes the human experience. What do we really know about this experience? Many scientific disciplines have developed over the last two hundred years for the purpose of discovering the mysteries of nature, but this search has only engendered new questions about the nature of existence. Yoga is a discipline or way of life designed to promote the physical, mental and spiritual development of the human being. It leads a person to discover the answers to the most important questions of life such as Who am I?, Why am I here? and Where am I going?

The literal meaning of the word YOGA is to *"YOKE"* or to *"LINK"* back. The implication is:

to link back to the original source, the original essence, that which transcends all mental and intellectual attempts at comprehension, but which is the essential nature of everything in CREATION. While in the strict or dogmatic sense, Yoga philosophy and practice is a separate discipline from religion, yoga and religion have been linked at many points throughout history. In a manner of speaking, Yoga as a discipline may be seen as a non-sectarian transpersonal science or practice to promote spiritual development and harmony of mind and body thorough mental and physical disciplines including meditation, psycho-physical exercises, and performing action with the correct attitude.

The disciplines of Yoga fall under five major categories. These are: *Yoga of Wisdom, Yoga of Devotional Love, Yoga of Meditation, Tantric Yoga* and *Yoga of Selfless Action.* Within these categories there are subsidiary forms which are part of the main disciplines. The important point to remember is that all aspects of yoga can and should be used in an integral fashion to effect an efficient and harmonized spiritual movement in the practitioner. Therefore, while there may be an area of special emphasis, other elements are bound to become part of the yoga program as needed. For example, while a yogin may place emphasis on the yoga of wisdom, they may also practice devotional yoga and meditation yoga along with the wisdom studies.

While it is true that yogic practices may be found in religion, strictly speaking, yoga is neither a religion or a philosophy. It should be thought of more as a way of life or discipline for promoting greater fullness and experience of life. Yoga was developed at the dawn of history by those who wanted more out of life. These special men and women wanted to discover the true origins of creation and of themselves. Therefore, they set out to explore the vast reaches of consciousness within themselves. They are sometimes referred to as "Seers", "Sages", etc. Awareness or consciousness can only be increased when the mind is in a state of peace and harmony. Thus, the disciplines of meditation (which are part of Yoga), and wisdom (the philosophical teachings for understanding reality as it is) are the primary means to controlling the mind and allowing the individual to mature psychologically and spiritually.

The teachings which were practiced in the Ancient Egyptian temples were the same ones later intellectually defined into a literary form by the Indian Sages of Vedanta and Yoga. This was discussed in our book *Egyptian Yoga: The Philosophy of Enlightenment*. The Indian Mysteries of Yoga and Vedanta represent an unfolding and intellectual exposition of the Egyptian Mysteries. Also, the study of Gnostic Christianity or Christianity before Roman Catholicism will be useful to our study since Christianity originated in Ancient Egypt and was also based on the Ancient Egyptian Mysteries. Therefore, the study of the Egyptian Mysteries, early Christianity and Indian Vedanta-Yoga will provide the most comprehensive teaching on how to practice the disciplines of Yoga leading to the attainment of Enlightenment.

The question is how to accomplish these seemingly impossible tasks? How to transform yourself and realize the deepest mysteries of existence? How to discover "who am I?" This is the mission of Yoga Philosophy and the purpose of yogic practices. Yoga does not seek to convert or impose religious beliefs on any one. Ancient Egypt was the source of civilization and the source of religion and Yoga. Therefore, all systems of mystical spirituality can coexist harmoniously within these teachings when they are correctly understood.

The goal of yoga is to promote integration of the mind-body-spirit complex in order to produce optimal health of the human being. This is accomplished through mental and physical exercises which promote the free flow of spiritual energy by reducing mental complexes caused by ignorance. There are two roads which human beings can follow, one of wisdom and the other of ignorance. The path of the masses is generally the path of ignorance which leads them into negative situations, thoughts and deeds. These in turn lead to ill health and sorrow in life. The other road is based on wisdom and it leads to health, true happiness and enlightenment.

Our mission is to extol the wisdom of yoga and mystical spirituality from the Ancient Egyptian perspective and to show the practice of the teachings through our books, videos and audio productions. You may find a complete listing of other books by the author, in the back of this volume.

How to study the wisdom teachings:

There is a specific technique which is prescribed by the scriptures themselves for studying the teachings, proverbs and aphorisms of mystical wisdom. The method is as follows:

The spiritual aspirant should read the desired text thoroughly, taking note of any particular teachings which resonates with him or her.

The aspirant should make a habit of collecting those teachings and reading them over frequently. The scriptures should be read and re-read because the subtle levels of the teachings will be increasingly understood the more the teachings are reviewed.

One useful exercise is to choose some of the most special teachings you would like to focus on and place them in large type or as posters in your living areas so as to be visible to remind you of the teaching.

The aspirant should discuss those teachings with others of like mind when possible because this will help to promote greater understanding and act as an active spiritual practice in which the teachings are kept at the forefront of the mind. In this way, the teachings can become an integral part of everyday life and not reserved for a particular time of day or of the week.

The study of the wisdom teachings should be a continuous process in which the teachings become the predominant factor of life rather than the useless and oftentimes negative and illusory thoughts of those who are ignorant of spiritual truths. This spiritual discipline should be observed until Enlightenment is attained.

May you discover supreme peace in this very lifetime!

MUATA ☉

(HETEP - Supreme Peace)

This Volume is Dedicated
to

Ptah

PART I
Shetau Akhet:
The Mysteries of Matter and the Phenomenal Universe

Ancient Egyptian Physics and Yoga

INTRODUCTION

The American Heritage Dictionary defines Physics as:

The science of matter and energy and of the interactions between the two.

The Random House Encyclopedia defines Physics as:

Physics, study and understanding of natural phenomena in terms of energy and matter. The scientific knowledge thus acquired is put to use by the technologist and engineer. The forms of energy studied include heat, light, mechanical, electrical, sound, and nuclear. The properties of matter itself and the interaction of these different energy forms with matter are also part of physics. It was thought that the properties of matter could be described completely by Newton's laws of motion and gravitation. Although large-scale systems are adequately explained so, classical physics must be replaced by quantum theory (1900) to describe the properties of atoms, etc., and by relativity (1905, 1915) to describe gravitational and very high velocity events.

In the last 100 years, the scientific community has developed entirely new concepts to understand the universe. Prior to the emergence of notable physicists such as Albert Einstein, the universe was thought to be a collection of physical objects with set properties and immutable existence.

With the introduction of the Quantum theory and the particle accelerator experiments that have proven it, a major revolution has occurred in the scientific community. No longer is the universe seen as a machine composed of intricate parts but as an wondrous collection of objects which are all interrelated and inseparable, whose underlying essence is one and the same: ENERGY.

This has been the revolutionary discovery by modern physicists, that the world as the human senses see it, is not at all what it really is under the rigorous examination of modern scientific instruments. Nature has been revealed to be an integrated entity which is guided by an intelligence which is beyond the grasp of science.

Does this sound familiar? Ancient Mystical Philosophers have stated that the world is an illusion from which humankind needs to wake up. From the Ancient Egyptian Pyramid texts to the Indian Upanishads, there are statements claiming that the universe is not what it appears to be to the human senses and mind.

Ancient philosophers and mystics discovered that the human mind and senses are too limited to see nature in its true form. For this reason they have compared ordinary human existence to a dream. However, when the human mind undergoes certain disciplines of purification of the thought process and the understanding of the teachings which come from those who have been successful in transcending their limited minds and senses, then an entirely new view of existence emerges. This is why the ancient sages 8,000 years ago in the Ancient Egyptian Pyramid texts proclaimed that we must "wake up" from the dreamlike state which most people consider to be "normal".

To the King:
May you awake in peace!
May you awake in peace!
May Taitet awake in peace!
{May} the Eye of Horus which is in Dep {awake} in peace!
May the Eye of Horus which is in the Mansions of the
Nt-crown awake in peace!

Pyramid Texts. Utterance 81

This is the basis of yoga. Ancient yogis discovered long ago that the essence of creation is a vast ocean of consciousness in different states of vibration. Modern physicists would call it a vast ocean of energy in different forms or states.

This theme of waking up will be elaborated in the book *The Mind of Set: Introduction to*

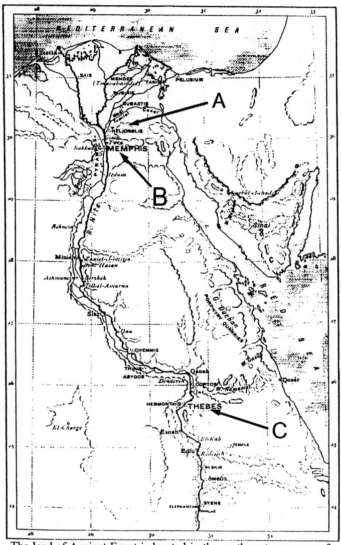

The land of Ancient Egypt is located in the north-eastern corner of the African Continent. The cities wherein the theology of the Trinity was developed are outlined as follows.

A- Anu (Heliopolis), B-Hetkaptah (Memphis), and C-Waset (Thebes).

Mystical Psychology in which we will explore the inner workings of the human mind. For now it is important for you to understand the true essence of creation. You must at this level intellectually grasp the idea that the universe, including all living beings (this includes you) is one unified existence. The sages of Ancient Egypt explained this intuitive view of creation in the Theology of Memphis whose main character is the deity called Ptah. Ptah is one of the names of the Supreme Being. Memphite Theology was the teaching given by the Ancient Egyptian priests of Memphis, Egypt. Memphite theology was chosen for inclusion in the book *Egyptian Yoga: The Philosophy of Enlightenment* because it most closely resembles the theory of modern physics.

However, there are several important Ancient Egyptian myths which explain the creation of the universe. All of them relate to each other and each explain different aspects of the underlying essence of the universe. All of them speak of the primordial ocean (Nu or Nun) of existence wherein there was no differentiation between objects. This means that there were no colors, no solid, gas and liquids, no multiplicity of life forms and no movement. Everything that exists now, and will ever exist in the future, existed in that primordial ocean. When the first being arose from that ocean as a thought in *the heart* (cosmic mind), that being assumed a name and the ocean immediately began assuming different forms according to the desire of the cosmic mind in much the same way that a dream arises out of the mind and assumes different forms. The idea of the Primeval Ocean later appears in the Christian Bible, in Hindu mythology and other religions.

It must be understood that all the elements discussed here, the cosmic mind, the primordial being, all of the objects that took form, were all contained in the primordial ocean in the beginning. Therefore, creation is not something that a being from the outside accomplishes. It is a change which occurs within already existing matter (Primeval Ocean). God is the ocean and the ocean appears as the outer manifestation of the universe. Therefore, the universe is the outer manifestation of God or Consciousness. Thus, according to Memphite Theology, God is the source, the underlying essence of creation as well as its manifestation. This Supreme Being has been called by several different Ancient Egyptian names: *Ptah, Amun, Ra, Osiris, Isis, Hathor, Neter, and all other Ancient Egyptian gods and goddesses.* Other religions have used other names to signify the same idea:

> The concept of the Absolute reality is embodied in the **NETER (NTR)** of Egypt, **Ntu** of the Yorubas, **Amma** of the Dogon, **Brahman** if Hinduism, the **Tao** of Taoism, the **Darmakaya** of Buddhism, **God-Kingdom of Heaven** of Christianity, **Kether** of the Kabbalah, the **Great Spirit and Quetzalcoatle** of Native Americans, and **Allah** of the Muslims.

The Egyptian Trinity mythology of *Amun-Ra-Ptah* represents a major philosophical discourse on the composition of nature. Memphite Theology, based on Ptah is only a third of the entire teaching. The entire wisdom of the Trinity, the deeper mystical implications of Memphite Theology and what it represents for the practice of yoga will be more fully discussed later in in this volume. Once again, the most important idea to understand now is that the universe is like an ocean of existence in which everything is alive and infused with the sustaining essence of the Divine (GOD).

In Memphite Theology, Ptah (God) is not seen as a creator who by some unnatural magic causes the universe to exist out of nothing. When it is stated that the universe was created by magic it is not the same magic performed by magicians. This kind of magic is like the magic by which salt dissolves into water. It seems to have disappeared, but when the water is evaporated the salt reappears. In the same way, Ptah is the hidden essence of creation and is the essence of the human soul which perceives the universe as well. Ptah has indeed become the Universe, or perhaps it would be more accurate to say that the universe appears as such to the untrained human mind, but to the enlightened yogi, he/she sees only God. Just as wind and its motion are one and the same, and the ocean and its waves are one and the same. The Supreme Self and the objects of the world are one and the same. According to Memphite Theology the world is composed of *neters*. These neters are divine energy forces which compose all physical phenomena. These neters have assumed the bodies (forms) of all the objects in the world which appear on the surface to be different and separate from each other, but in reality, the neters are the essence of God and therefore God has entered into all forms of existence.

In Chapter 17 of the *Egyptian Book of Coming Forth By Day,* the same statement about the Supreme Being manifesting as the neters, or forms of nature, is found.

...Ra is the creator of the names of his limbs; have come into existence these in the form of the Neters...(Ch. 17:10-11)

All existence occurs in a range of vibration from subtle to gross. Consciousness is the subtlest form of existence and it therefore permeates all other objects. Next in level of subtlety is the Spirit and it is Consciousness that directs the Spirit to enliven a particular body (neter). Therefore, Spirit is the vivifier (life giver) or mover behind the gross objects of the world. For this reason a dead body does not perceive after death. The spirit has left it at the command of Consciousness or the soul.

Above: The Creation, Ra-Kheper emerging out of the primeval ocean, NU.

> *"In the form of Khepra, Ra (NETER) declares that*
> *before him, nothing existed; Time, Space, the realm*
> *of matter, Nun, the primeval waters (unformed*
> *mater) did not exist. His power was not exhausted by*
> *that single creative act; he continued to create mil-*
> *lions and millions of new forms out of that which he*
> *had already created."*

The same great truth which is the main teaching of Memphite Theology, that the various objects and life forms of creation are in reality forms assumed by God, is also embodied in the *Book of Coming Forth By Day*. One prominent example of this teaching is found in Chapter 83, *The Chapter of Changing Into a Bennu* (Phoenix). In it the initiate utters words of power which affirm that the underlying essence of creation is one and the same: God. Further, the utterance explains that Neter (God) is present in all of the various life forms and objects.

> I came into existence from un-
> formed matter; I created myself in
> the image of the God Khepera,
> and I grew in the form of plants. I
> am hidden in the likeness of the
> Tortoise. I am the essence of every
> god and goddess. I am the origin
> of the four quarters of the world. I
> am the seventh of those seven
> *Urei* who came into existence in
> the East. I am the mighty one Ho-
> rus who illumines the world with
> his person. I am God in the like-

Left: Sekhmet, the consort of Ptah.

Right: Nefertem, the son of Ptah and Sekhmet.

Along with Ptah Sekhmet and Nefertem constitute the Trinity of Hetkaptah, the city of the Ka of Ptah and therefore they are a symbol of the three principles of creation in much the same way as Osiris, Isis and Horus.

Below left: The Forms of Nefertem.

Below right: Horus on the Lotus of Creation.

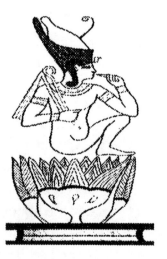

ness of Set and Tehuti who dwelleth among us in the Judgment of Him who dwells in Sekhem, and of the spirits of Anu. I sail among them , and I come; I am crowned. I have become a shining one-glorious. I am mighty. I am holy among the gods and goddesses...

Order of subtlety of matter in creation:

Pure Consciousness The Universal Soul (most subtle)	Individual Soul	Mind and Senses	Gross Physical Bodies

▷▷▷▷▷▷▷▷▷▷▷▷▷▷▷▷▷▷▷▷▷▷▷▷

One of the reasons why this wisdom has been held to be a *mystery* is that it defies proof by the human senses. If you look at a flower, a rock, your skin, or into space, you do not see swirling energy or a homogeneous mass of matter; you see objects composed of different textures, mass, colors, etc., and this seemingly proper evidence collected by your senses is what you accept to be real. Yet modern science has proven that it is not real.

This is because your senses are limited in their perceptive capacity and your mind is conditioned to accept and process only certain kinds of information. What if you had the eyes of a hawk, or the olfactory capacity of a hound dog? Your perceptions of reality would be quite different. Therefore, you must not accept the information gathered from your senses as being reflective of reality as it truly is.

This is why the ancient Sages have developed disciplines by which you are able to separate yourself from your mind and senses and to thereby discover the essence of reality by transcending the mind and sense in order to perceive reality directly, without obstruction or distortion. Once you fully understand this teaching you will be ready to reflect on it. This process of reflection wherein you continuously think about it, causes it to gradually sink deeper and deeper into your mind until the illusion is finally broken. This is known as intuitional realization of the Self or Enlightenment. You transcend the mind and senses and use intuition to understand your true essence which is divine and the same as the essence of the universe. This is the key to making the teachings of

The Atom

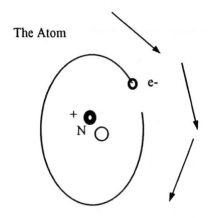

Until recently, modern science considered that matter was an abiding substance, that it exists for ever as matter. However experiments in quantum physics have shown that matter and energy are interchangeable. Therefore, matter, in its various forms, is illusory and "unreal".

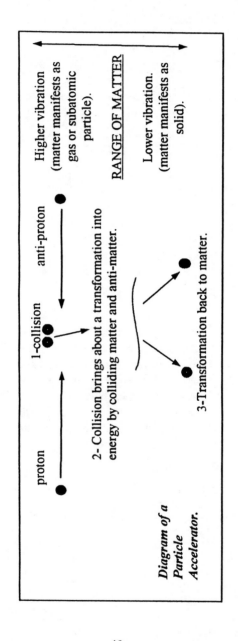

Higher vibration (matter manifests as gas or subatomic particle).

RANGE OF MATTER

Lower vibration. (matter manifests as solid).

anti-proton

1-collision

proton

2- Collision brings about a transformation into energy by colliding matter and anti-matter.

3-Transformation back to matter.

Diagram of a Particle Accelerator.

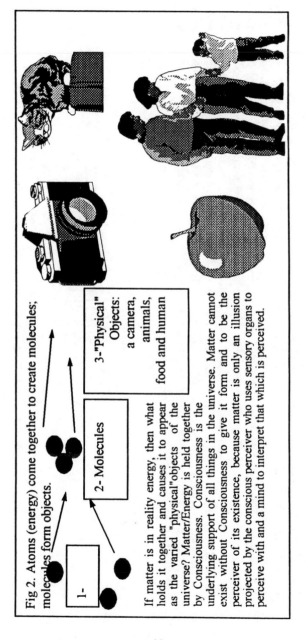

Fig 2. Atoms (energy) come together to create molecules; molecules form objects.

1-

2- Molecules

3-"Physical" Objects: a camera, animals, food and human

If matter is in reality energy, then what holds it together and causes it to appear as the varied "physical"objects of the universe? Matter/Energy is held together by Consciousness. Consciousness is the underlying support of all things in the universe. Matter cannot exist without Consciousness to give it form and to be the perceiver of its existence, because matter is only an illusion projected by the conscious perceiver who uses sensory organs to perceive with and a mind to interpret that which is perceived.

The Diagrams on this series of pages show the findings of modern science. It has been proven that all objects in creation, that is all matter, is composed of the same material. Further, that "material" or "essence" is called energy in modern physics. However, ancient Mystical philosophy calls it Consciousness and it is pure, undifferentiated Consciousness which underlies every object as well as all life in creation. It may be said that undifferentiated Consciousness is transcendental and possessing every potential to "become" any object. When this transformation from undifferentiated to differentiated occurs, then the spirit is said to have come into being. However, this coming into being is not a permanent occurrence, as modern science has proven that matter can go back to energy and then become matter again.. If this were so, there would be no way to transcend the solidity of gross, physical existence. Thus, it is possible to discover increasingly more subtle levels of one's own consciousness and thereby, become "enlightened to the undifferentiated, transcendental realm of existence even while occupying the gross form of a human body. When this movement in spiritual awareness reaches the heights of self-discovery it is referred to as "*Nehas-t*", the resurrection.

Above: Waves of energy are particles and particles are also waves. Both are energy in different forms.

42

mystical philosophy come true in your life. Once you learn the teachings intellectually you must then practice them intensively under proper guidance. Otherwise they only remain at the intellectual level of mind and there is no intuitional realization of the truth.

"The Universe is Mental" - This statement is one of the most important ideas given in Memphite Theology. It is of paramount importance to the understanding of mystical philosophy. The original act of creation occurred with the first thought. After this thought occurred, the organs of action carried out the actual creative acts which caused matter to appear as various objects of creation. In much the same way that a human being thinks an idea and then speaks it or moves an organ of action (eye, arm, etc.) to cause the idea to manifest, God has created the world by having it as an idea in the cosmic mind and then projecting that idea in the form of neters or cosmic forces.

The original thought, however, is the most important factor because it is the thought which causes the idea and the manifestation to exist. In the same way that you produce an entire world of thoughts, as well as the bodies and objects by which your thoughts manifest and interact when you dream, God has caused this world of time and space to exist and manifest the thoughts of the Self (God).

Since the essence of your existence is God, YOU are constantly manifesting a particular form of will. If you are caught up in a state of ignorance and do not have awareness of your divine connection to God you will think and manifest egoistic values. Your desires may or may not come to pass as you would like them. In this condition you will experience either partial fulfillment of your desires or disappointment when your desires do not come true. This is the condition of the masses of people. Even though they are supported by the Divine Self for their existence, they are unaware of that support and believe themselves to be individual personalities (this is the state of egoism, another term used is the state of ignorance). They are lead by their egoistic thoughts and desires. If you were able to discover and align yourself with the cosmic mind, then you would think thoughts which are in line with cosmic will and these would always come true because these

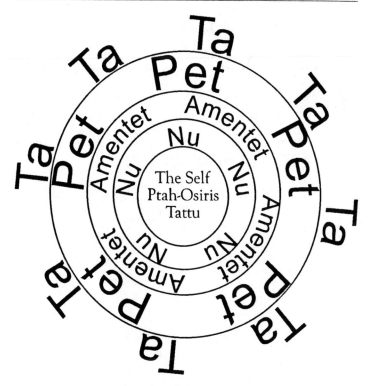

Above: a two dimensional schematic drawing of creation and its relationship to the Self or Soul, based on Ancient Egyptian mystical philosophy.

The Ancient Egyptian concept of creation includes three realms. These are the TA, ⎯⎯ ⵣ (Earth), Pet, ⵣ◻◦ (Heaven), and the Ṭuat ★🐍◻ ⬱🦶 (the Netherworld - Amenta, Astral plane).

All realms originate from the Self and are created by temporarily (period of billions of years in human terms) transforming subtle matter (undifferentiated consciousness) into gross matter (the physical world-neteru).

thoughts are the desires of God. In the following lessons you will learn how to discover the will of God as it is flowing through you. You have a special role to play in the cosmic drama of the world process. As you learn the art of playing that role you will become more in touch with your cosmic nature and achieve oneness with it (YOGA-Enlightenment).

PART II
The Mystical Philosophy of Matter in Modern Physics and The Ancient Egyptian Inscription of Shabaka.

Modern Physics

Modern Physics appears to be "proving" Ancient Mystical Philosophy. In the past 20 years, studies that have tried to find the smallest particle or to explore the outer limits of space have come up with answers which support the ancient mystical philosophical view of the cosmos and the constitution of the human being.

Science is discovering that the Universe is infinite in all directions, both at the atomic (micro) level and at the planetary (macro) level. It is also finding that what we call "matter", is not what it appears to be. In fact, studies suggest that matter is 99.9% empty space surrounded by an idea (information, thought), consciousness. Contrary to popular belief, quantum physicists have found that they cannot explain what matter is nor what holds it together. The remaining .1% of matter which appears to be visible is also theorized by quantum physics (modern physics) to be an optical illusion. The "atom" is said to be composed of a positively (+) charged "Particle" called a "proton" and a particle with no charge (N), called a "neutron", in the center. These two particles are said to be surrounded by an electron which carries a negative (-) charge and revolves around the nucleus. All matter is found to be composed of the same protons, neutrons and electrons. The difference in appearance comes from the different numbers of "particles" in each "atom" and also from the combination of different atoms with varied combinations of the three particles. Further, it is known that electrons have no weight and that there is a vast "empty space" between the protons and the electrons that circulate around them; also that there is "empty space" inside of the protons, neutrons and electrons. Therefore, what we are seeing and touching by use of our senses is not at all what it appears to be.

What we seem to perceive with our senses is in reality, only different aspects of the same substance. That is, when energy "vibrates" at a high speed (frequency) it appears as a light (less dense, less weight) material such as gas or electricity. When it "vibrates" at a lower speed it appears as a solid (dense material) object such as rocks or metal. The higher the vibrations are, the more subtle the "material" will appear to be. The slower the vibrations are, the more solid, rigid and static it will appear to be. When matter vibrates at very high rates, it goes beyond the gaseous state; then matter appears as rays such as sun-rays or X-rays. At higher rates of vibration, it would be so subtle that it could fit in between the "empty spaces" in the slower vibrating matter. It could pass through it or "reside" in it. This is the subtle realm of the "spirit" body which "permeates" the "physical" body. The object of all spiritual movements is to "identify" one's consciousness, one's concept of who one is, with the "subtlest reality" rather than with the gross physical reality because the physical one is perishable and transient, whereas the subtlest one is transcendental, immortal and all-pervasive. In fact, it is the "subtle" spirit from which "gross" matter is created. For this reason, keeping a "light" lifestyle which promotes higher mental vibrations, a "light" diet and "light" thoughts are important as will be seen in further chapters.

The new generation of physicists beginning with Albert Einstein have developed a "new physics." They now believe that matter, that is, everything which can be perceived with our senses, including our bodies, is an

"ILLUSION." If we were to look at matter with an electron microscope in an attempt to see it the way it truly is, you would see structures that appear as small planets and moons circling them at lightning speeds. Even the most solid looking structures are really moving; everything is in perpetual motion. Further, we would see that matter seems to come out of nowhere and then goes back into "nowhere-ness." As all "matter" is composed of the same "stuff," the different objects we see in the world are merely different combinations of the same material substance common to all things; this is what is meant by an illusion or appearance of multiplicity and variety. The "new physics" says that matter is nothing more than energy.

Particle accelerator experiments attempted to break down atoms into smaller units by colliding them at great speeds. Scientists found that when a positively charged proton (matter) and a negatively charged proton (anti-matter) are crashed together, particles turned into energy (wave patterns) and then back to matter again. Energy and matter are therefore, interchangeable. This interchangeability of matter and energy is represented in Einstein's famous formula $E=mc^2$ who initially developed this theory mentally (without experimentation). Therefore, even the most solid looking objects are in reality ENERGY in motion at different vibratory rates.

Further, modern science has discovered that even objects of the world which appear to be separate, such as human beings, are in reality "exchanging pieces of each other" on a continuous basis. That is to say, every time we breathe out we are expelling atoms and molecules from our internal organs. Therefore, every time we breathe, we are sharing pieces of our bodies with other people and with the environment. For example, air that is breathed by someone in India may be breathed by someone in the United States two days later and vice versa. Thus, the physical world which appears to have defined boundaries is only an illusion. In reality, the world is one interrelated mass of atoms and energy which is being "caused" to move and interact by some seemingly "unknown" force.

The Ancient Mystical Philosophy of an all encompassing "force" that binds the universe together was espoused thousands of years ago in the Egyptian philosophy of SEKHEM, the Indian idea of PRANA, the Chinese idea of CHI and in the philosophies of other cultures. Philosophy further states that this "FORCE" can be controlled through mental discipline. Modern science has now, based on scientific evidence, postulated the existence of a substance called *"DARK MATTER"* which is described as an "unseen, unfelt substance that makes up to 99% of the Universe." This means that not only is the world one interrelated mass, but that it is a part of the greater mass called the "Universe".

This theory supports the ancient philosophical idea that the "created" Universe really does not exist except as perceived through the mind of the individual. It is a manifestation of the Supreme Being that ebbs and flows in a time frame that encompasses an untold number (perhaps billions) of years. It is "created" and "destroyed" periodically. This supports the theory of a *"BIG BANG"* and the *"Expanding-Contracting Model of the Universe."* The last "Creation" is thought by scientists to have occurred several billions of years ago. In the future, they theorize that the universe will close in on itself (contract), and all the planets, stars, etc. will return to one point, as represented by the point in the symbol of Ra, ☉.

Then, a new "creation" or big bang will occur again. This is the same information stated in age old philosophical scriptures dating from the beginning of "historical" times.

Those who are alive now will not witness that "dissolution" since it is theorized that it will not occur for millions of years in the future, however, the implications of what it means are crucial to the understanding of the nature of reality (the cosmos) with which humans are intimately related. In fact, Ancient Mystical Philosophy states that the "Created" universe is only an appearance for the generation of a stage upon which the human experience may occur. In addition, this "illusion" that has been created by our conditioned minds is a "reality" only to the extent that we "believe" in it.

Thus, reality appears to be a relative idea. Ancient Mystical Philosophy states that the true essence of things can be seen by the liberated mind which sees what lies beyond the information given by the senses and that those whose minds are not liberated will experience the "physical" world as if it really "exists." For example, there is no blue sky, it only appears to be blue because of the limited human sense of vision. Also, you are not stationary just because you are standing still. Our planet, a ball of "mud" we call earth, is flying through the universe at thousands of miles per hour and spinning at hundreds of miles per hour. Yet as you function on a daily basis this realization probably does not cross your mind, because it is not being perceived by your senses.

Modern science has now accepted that so called "physical reality" cannot exist outside of the person conducting the experiments. An older theory held that the person conducting the experiment could be considered separate and apart from the phenomena being observed. Modern science now holds that nature and all phenomena occur because of an experimenter's ability to conceptualize the phenomena and to interpret it. Therefore, the observer is part of the phenomena being observed. Consequently, modern science now uses a new term for the experimenter. The new term is <u>participant.</u>

Thus, the experimenter is really a participant in the experiment because his or her consciousness conceives, determines, perceives, interprets and understands it. No experiment or observed phenomena in nature can occur without someone to conceive that something is happening, determine that something is happening, perceive that something is happening (through instruments or the senses), and finally to interpret what has happened and to understand that interpretation. Therefore, the most recent theory in modern physics is that matter, that is to say Creation, is composed of not only energy in varying degrees of density (vibration), but that it is "intelligent", or it might be better understood by saying that matter and energy are manifestations of Cosmic Intelligence (consciousness).

The Illusion of Time According to The Teaching of Mer-Ka-Re

Einstein's theory of relativity showed that time is not a constant, fixed, and tangible factor to which we are so accustomed. In fact, the concept of time depends on the perception of the individual who is experiencing the passage of time. The very fact that time does not have a fixed point of reference is acknowledge by physicists to be a factor of its illusoriness. The concept of time developed out of a need to explain the way in which events seem to occur in a sequential manner, but modern physics has proven this idea to be an illusion of the human mind. In fact what we seem to experience is not the passage of time, but the motion of the neters (opposite but complementary forces) as they (we) interact with each other. The neters (cosmic energies and elements) are ever engaged in perpetual change which the human mind confuses as the passage of time. Einstein was not the first to state a theory of relativity. The theory of time relativity was stated in Ancient Egyptian spiritual texts and later in Indian spiritual texts thousands of years before Einstein. In the following text, *"Instruction to Mer-ka-Ré"*, a pharaoh teaches his son about the importance of performing righteous actions in this lifetime because he will be judged by the assessors of Maat who exist in a different time reference than the one which is known of by ordinary humans:

"You know that they are not merciful the day when they judge the miserable one..... Do not count on the passage of

the years; they consider a lifetime as but an hour. After death man remains in existence and his acts accumulate beside him. Life in the other world is eternal, but he who arrives without sin before the Judge of the Dead, he will be there as a Neter and he will walk freely as do the masters of eternity"

Creation, Matter and Physical Reality According to the *Shabaka Stone* Inscription.

The nature and composition of *"matter"* or what is termed *"physical reality"* and the concept of *"consciousness"* were understood and clearly set down in the hieroglyphic texts which date back to 5,500 B.C.E in the theological system of Memphis, Egypt as follows:

In the beginning only NETER (GOD of Gods) existed and nothing else. Then Neter became three, Amon - Ra - Ptah.

The *"Shabaka Stone"* states:
"Ptah conceived in his heart (reasoning consciousness) all that would exist and at his utterance (the word - will, power to make manifest), created Nun, the

primeval waters (unformed matter-energy).

Then, not having a place to sit Ptah causes Nun to emerge from the primeval waters as the Primeval Hill so that he may have a place to sit. Atom then emerges and sits upon Ptah. Then came out of the waters four pairs of Gods, the Ogdoad (eight Gods):

Nun (primeval waters) and Nunet (heaven).
Huh (boundlessness) and Huhet (that which has boundaries).
Kuk (darkness) and Kuket (light).
Amon (the hidden) and Amonet (that which is manifest).

The Neters (Nun, Nunet, Huh, Huhet, Kuk, Kuket, Amon, Amonet) are the lips and teeth of (GOD'S) mouth which speaks the names of all things which come into existence . . .

. . . The Heart and tongue have power over all the limbs. GOD is found as the heart within all bodies, and in the mouth

of each Neter and all humans as the tongue (will), of all things that live. . . It is GOD who thinks (as the Heart) and who commands (as the tongue). . .

. . . That which the nose breathes, the eyes see, the ears hear; all of these (senses) are communicated to the heart. It is the heart (mind) which makes all knowledge and awareness manifest, and then the tongue is what repeats what the heart has thought. . .

. . . All divine utterances manifested themselves through the thoughts of the heart and the commandments of the tongue. . .

. . . Justice is done to they who do what is loved, punishment to they who do what is hated. Life is given to they who are peaceful, death is given to the criminal. . .

. . .In truth GOD caused the Neters to be born, the creation of the cities, establishment of the nomes, the establishment of the Neters in their places of adoration. . .

. GOD made their likenesses according to their desire. Thereby, the Neters entered into their bodies, the variety of wood, all types of mineral, clay, and all things that grow from these and in which they have taken place, foods, provisions, and all good things... He (Ptah) is Horus. "

Thus, through the Shabaka Inscription, we are instructed in the following wisdom:

1- Creation came into being through the mind (thought) of Ptah (the GOD of Gods) and his utterance (power).

2- GOD created "Energy - Matter" (Nun), and then formed the principals by which they would be governed (four pairs of opposites).

3- Atom (Sun and Fire God) performs the work of creation by sitting on Ptah, taking the creative thought, and then acting on the command of GOD. Therefore, "ATOMS" are the creative thought from GOD which "obey" GOD'S will, i.e. **_EXISTENCE._** GOD gives existence; human consciousness allows perception of and gives meaning to that existence.

4- GOD is conscious of creation, therefore, creation exists.

5- Consciousness, the "HEART", (what modern physics would call "intelligence"), is the underlying reality behind all existence and all human experience. The senses receive the information from the environment and thereby, register knowledge and existence. In fact, the world (creation) exists because consciousness (soul-intelligence) projects its existence through thought power. There can be no existence without consciousness to perceive it. GOD IS the Neters and the Neters are creation.

6- Horus and Ptah are one in the same.

The understanding that GOD is located within the "bodies of all things" is also found in the ancient Yoga text of India called *"Yoga Vasistha"* (first recorded in c. 750 A.C.E.):

"Just as there is butter in every kind of milk, similarly the Supreme abides in the bodies of all things."

Thus, the universe is mental as is stated by the God Tehuti-Hermes:

"The Universe is Mental, they who grasp the mental nature of the universe are far along the path of self mastery."

Creation itself is **THOUGHT** and it is sustained by **THOUGHT** power. Another name for the God Tehuti-Hermes (God of writing, wisdom and scribe of the Gods) is Thoth. The similarity of the word "Thoth" to the word "thought" is striking since Thoth (thought) is the determiner of fate in the karmic scales of MAAT. Thoth represents the mind. Mental advancement (raising consciousness, understanding) is the key to understanding creation.

7- GOD is the underlying reality (consciousness) behind all events of the world . GOD is that which is perceived and also the perceiver. Therefore, only GOD exists. Nature does not exist as a separate entity from GOD. The soul of all things is GOD (NETER).

8- GOD is the underlying reality (consciousness) behind all objects that exist (wood, minerals, foods, provisions, and all things that come from these).

9- The doctrine of life (mental peace) and death (criminal behavior - mental unrest).

BASIC EGYPTIAN PHYSICS:

5
NETERS

NETERS = Creation of elements (air, fire, water, earth), different objects with name and form arise because of the interaction of different elements which are themselves composed of the same thing-consciousness). Creation of the qualities of matter - hot, dry, wet, cold, etc., the physical and astral universe which is composed of matter in various degrees of vibrational existence from gross (solid-lower frequency) to subtle (waves-higher frequency).

4
ATOM

Under the direction of Ptah, Atom creates all things. Neters, qualities of matter. Atom (the will-power to create) who is both male and female, does the will of Ptah (mind).

3
NUN

Formed matter devoid of will to become anything in particular.

2
PTAH (HORUS)

Mind-Consciousness, creates all (100%) matter
through thought - first condensed matter (Nun-
unformed matter-energy).

1
NETER

(Nameless One, Hidden One, Formless One,
Self-existent Being, intangible, beyond time and
space, pure consciousness, intelligence underlying and supporting all matter).

**The Mind of GOD Conceives Creation as a
Dream Within a Dream**

From the Ancient Egyptian Scriptures...

> *"In the form of Khepera, Ra
> (NETER) declares that before
> him, nothing existed; Time,
> Space, the realm of matter, Nun,
> the primeval waters (unformed
> mater) did not exist. His power
> was not exhausted by that single*

creative act; he continued to create millions and millions of new forms out of that which he had already created."

Just as a dream can be experienced within another dream, GOD creates new forms of existence (world systems, universes, life forms, etc.) as successive mental thoughts within thoughts. Modern physics would see this concept as a multi-dimensional movement of energy. Energy is neither used nor wasted, only reformulated into ever changing infinity. In one of the most important, but not well known ancient Indian Vedantic texts called *"Yoga Vasistha"*, also known as *"Maha Ramayana"*, there is a story illustrating the same idea of creation as expressed by GOD in the form of Khepra. A seeker of enlightenment meditates on his own existence and finds that he is meditating upon someone who is having a dream. The dream subject being meditated on discovers he is a dream of someone else and so on until the root personality or subject is reached. That root personality is GOD. In the same way we exist through many incarnations creating the projection of a body and a surrounding world but in reality each of us is GOD having innumerable dreams. In the *Yoga Vasistha* as well as the creation of Khepera, creation occurs due to the power of the mind to think and believe in what is thought. Since the universe proceeds from the mind of GOD, through a dream process as it were, it follows that all things, our mental ideas as well as what is called physical reality, are in reality, emanations from the cosmic mind of GOD. Therefore, it follows that attunement of the individual human mind with that cosmic mind will bring forth union with the cosmos (Maat). Thus, by getting back to the source of the original thoughts of the mind, it is possible to find enlightenment. This task may be accomplished by simple but intense reflection on the nature of reality. As we are innately divine neters (gods and goddesses), we too can create with our mind, not only ideas but new physical realities as well, through the practice and exercise of our heart (mind) and tongue (will). It is only because we have been convinced by the world that we are puny animals in need of salvation and assistance from outside of ourselves that we exist in a degraded, depressed state. Therefore, from an even higher perspective, it must be understood that our concepts of GOD, the cosmic mind that creates and causes existence to appear to exist, is only a projection of GOD.

Thus the mind of NETER, GOD, is the source of all creations, and everything that springs forth from them. This is the mystery of mysteries that must be known, not only "intellectually", but intuitionally. All philosophical, religious and scientific ideas originate from this one source. All other mysteries or ideas are only lower mysteries which proceed from within this simple truth. The pursuit of intricate religious, philosophical or mystical systems is thus likened to a dream within a dream, the pursuit of an illusion if they do not lead to this simple truth. As Creation is vast and capable of providing the mind with endless subjects and intricacies, it is easy to get caught in "illusions." Therefore, the most important ability to develop is *"the ability to distinguish the real from the unreal."* It is important therefore, to understand that spiritual freedom cannot be attained from reading the material in this or any other book. The information is needed but the goal goes beyond thoughts, so if a person thinks "I read the wisdom book so now I am enlightened," then that person is probably not truly enlightened. Enlightenment is not something one can "read" or "think"; it's something one <u>KNOWS.</u> When spiritual transformation occurs, there will be no question about what it is or how it feels. It has nothing to do with egoistic feelings of superiority over others due to one's "high wisdom" or other delusions of self-importance. It is however more like waking up in the morning and realizing one had a vivid dream which seemed "so real" but upon waking up (enlightenment), the dream of life disappears and there is a new reality, a wonderful reality beyond any past imaginings, a reality which transcends any notions of one's individual self.

Ancient philosophy tells us that the creation story is re-played every moment of every day. Every time our heart beats, a new moment of life is created. Everyday the sun rises, another day is created. Modern science agrees with this assessment. In less than one year, 98% of all the atoms in the human body are replaced with completely new ones. In less than a year and a half we have a completely new body. Therefore, the body and brain do not meet the criteria of reality as that which is unchanging. They are ever changing and illusory. They, along with the mind, are changeable with time. Therefore, the only reality is that which sustains them, that which keeps them working and allows them to have the illusion that they really exist. The only unchanging reality is the spirit.

The meaning of the word "PHYSICS" is "the study of the composition of Nature". The word "Nature" comes from the Ancient Latin word *"NATURA"*. The word *"Natura"* originates in the Egyptian words *"NETER"* (GOD) and *"NETERU"* (GOD'S manifestations). The early Greek students of physics, such as Thales and Democritus, learned the science of the study of GOD from the Egyptian masters who instructed them to *"Know Thyself"*. Since each human being is a neter, a manifestation of GOD, the most direct way to know GOD (NETER) is to study GOD'S manifestation, NETERU - ONESELF, because NETERU cannot exist without being sustained at every moment by NETER. Therefore, NETER can be found in NETERU. It is only due to the rampant, untrained thought processes that control the direction of the mind, that GOD (NETER) is not perceived by us (Neteru). Therefore, the study of NETER through NETER'S manifestations in NETERU requires the mastery of our thought faculty, Tehuti, and the understanding of laws by which nature exists (MAAT).

From Memphite theology (5,000 B.C.E.) we learned that the neters are in reality the myriad of forms which Ptah (GOD) assumes. Therefore, the idea of explaining the physical world was set forth in terms of principles (neters), represented by objects, personalities or animals, which exhibit and exemplify certain characteristics and tendencies that are found in nature as well as in human beings. This differs from the traditional western view of explaining the physical (material) world in terms of it being a concrete, absolute reality composed of "elements" because, according to the ancient scriptures, there is only one element that exists: GOD. Through philosophical examination and modern scientific experimentation, that idea of the world being an absolute reality is found to be illusory. Thus, the laws of existence by which the "physical" universe manifests and works is understood as interactions of opposite but complementary principles (Horus and Set).

There were three major Trinity systems in Ancient Egypt and all encompassed the symbolic form of Father, Mother and Child. These were: Osiris-Isis-Horus, Amun-Mut-Khons and Ptah-Sekhmet-Nefertem. In Ancient Egypt, the Trinities were not seen as being in contradiction with one another. Rather in Memphite Theology as in the other systems, the mystical interpretation of the three principles were seen as a metaphorical interpretation of the nature of Creation and the force which engenders it and sustains it. Thus, Ptah is the source and support of Creation. Sekhmet is the dynamic aspect or the power of Ptah and Nefer-tem refers to the beautiful (nefer) new life which emerges daily as the new day (tem - relating to Atem-Atom). The main symbol of Nefertem is the Lotus. He is the lotus of Creation which emerges out of the primeval waters (Nu). This is the same lotus upon which Horus sits. Therefore, the names of the characters in the Trinity of Memphis (Ptah-Sekhmet-Nefertem) relate to a profound understanding of the nature of Creation.

The Planes of Existence: The Mystical Code of The Trinity

The first sophisticated system of religion and yoga mystical philosophy in historical times occurred in Ancient Egypt. This system included all of the gods and goddesses which in later times became individually popular in various cities throughout Ancient Egypt. At the heart of this system of gods and goddesses was *Shetai*, the hidden and unmanifest essence of the universe, also known as *Nebertcher* and *Amun*. The system of religion of Ancient Egypt was called *Shetaut Neter* or the *Hidden Way of The Unmanifest Supreme Being*.

The term "unmanifest" relates to the fact that the Ancient Egyptians realized the illusory nature of physical reality. The phenomenal world, as it is perceived by the ordinary senses in a human being, is not the absolute reality of existence. In modern times, Quantum Physics experiments have uncovered the fact that "physical matter" is not "physical" at all, that it is "energy" in various states of manifestation or vibration. Thus, the Ancient Egyptians discovered that the phenomenal universe is only a "manifest" form which arises from a deeper,

The Forms of Ptah

unmanifest source. This notion was extensively explained in *Memphite Theology**. The theory of relativity relating to time and space was also expressed in the Ancient Egyptian creation stories long before Albert Einstein proposed his theory of relativity. *(See *Egyptian Yoga: The Philosophy of Enlightenment*)

The entire system of mystical philosophy of the hidden Supreme Being, as well as the method through which that Being manifests in the form of the phenomenal physical universe and individual human consciousness, was explained in progressive stages in the theology of the Trinity known as *Amun-Ra-Ptah*, which was said to have arisen out of the Supreme Being: *Nebertcher*. As Ancient Egyptian history moved on through thousands of years, each segment of this Trinity was adopted by a particular priesthood and locality which then set about to explain and expound the philosophy of that particular segment of the Trinity. The priests of the Ancient Egyptian city of *Anu* adopted Ra, the priesthood of the Ancient Egyptian city of *Hetkaptah* adopted Ptah, and the Ancient Egyptian city of *Weset or Newt* (Thebes) adopted Amun.

PART III

The Mystical Meaning of the Name of Ptah and its Relation to Neteru (Creation)

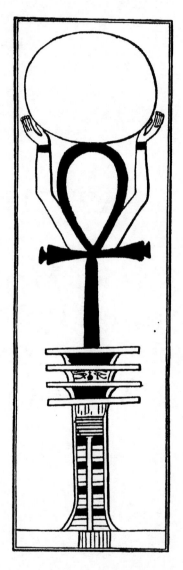

Above: The Tet, from which proceeds Life (Ankh),
arms supporting the Solar Disk.

The following formula constitutes the deeper teaching given in the mythology surrounding Ptah. The name of Ptah is written in hieroglyphic as a human form supporting heaven and earth. The name *Ptah* is composed of the following parts:

Pt = *"heaven"*,
ta = *"earth"*,
h = *as in heh* - *"support"*

Ptah is known as the *"Overlord of the two lands"* (Lower Egypt and Upper Egypt), also material existence (manifest) and spiritual (unmanifest). *Htp* is also the name of *PTAH (Pth)* if written backwards. He is also known as *Hetepi* ▭ ⅃⅃. Thus, Ptah (NETER, God, Horus) is the support of heaven and earth and the supreme abode of peace which transcends the realm of time and space and the pairs of opposites. In this aspect, Ptah is associated with *Shu*, the God of air and breath, who is therefore, the separator of heaven and earth (soul and body).

It is important to note that the symbol for God is one (ٱ) and nature is three (ٱٱٱ). This is a reference, in symbolic form, to the statement, *I became from God one, gods three.* Thus, God one, non-dual, unborn and eternal, beyond time and space, at the same time expressing as the Trinity, encompassing the phenomenal universe of time and space wherein there is a triad of consciousness and wherein everything experiences birth and death.

Another important feature of Memphite Theology is that the conception of Ptah is not of the physical (body) manifestation of the universe, as it is stated in utterance 33 of the Hymns of Amun: *He whose name is hidden is Amun, Ra belongeth to him as His face, and the body is Ptah.* This is because in Memphis, Ptah assumed the attributes and characteristics of the Supreme and Absolute Being. Thus, in this respect, the Theology of Memphis and the Theology of Thebes should not be confused. In Memphite Theology, Ptah is the substratum, the source and origination of creation. Creation is a thought in the mind of Ptah.

This principle of supremacy exists in the theology of each of the other members of the Trinity as well as in the centers (cities) of worship for other major Deities such as Isis, Horus, Hathor, etc. This is sometimes referred to as the principle of the "High God" within a given theological system. In this manner, the Ancient Egyptian neters can be looked at as being part of a theology which is local to their main cities of worship as well as being part of a national (within Ancient Egypt) and universal or international (outside Ancient Egypt) system of theology.

Examples of Local Theologies:

Ptah-Sekhmet-Nefertem
Amun-Mut-Khons
Ra-Nut-Geb

Examples of Universal Theologies:

Amun - Ra - Ptah
Osiris-Isis-Horus.

Thus, the Ancient Egyptian system of gods and goddesses has a local or national reference

Diagram A: A Summary of Memphite Theology depicting the Ancient Egyptian Hieroglyphic symbols of each creative principle:

NETERS

↑

ATUM (ATOM)

↑

NUN

↑

PTAH (HORUS)

↑

NETER
(The Supreme, Nameless, Transcendental Self)

Diagram A-2: A Summary of Memphite Theology depicting the attributes of each principle and their interrelationships:

NETERS

NETERS = Creation of elements (air, fire, water, earth); different objects with name and form arise because of the interaction of different elements which are themselves composed of the same thing-consciousness. Creation of the qualities of matter - hot, dry, wet, cold, etc., the physical and astral universes which are composed of matter in various degrees of vibrational existence from gross (solid-lower frequency) to subtle (waves-higher frequency).

ATUM (ATOM)

Under the direction of Ptah, Atom creates all things, neters, qualities of matter. Atom (the will-power to create) who is both male and female, does the will of Ptah (mind).

NUN

Formed matter devoid of will to become anything in particular.

PTAH (HORUS)

Mind-Consciousness, creates all (100%) matter through thought - first condensed matter (Nun- unformed matter-energy).

NETER

(Nameless One, Hidden One, Formless One, Self-existent Being, intangible, beyond time and space, pure consciousness, intelligence underlying and supporting all matter).

to specific nomes or cities within Ancient Egypt while at the same time being part of the all-encompassing Trinity system which became so popular that it was adopted outside of Egypt and became the basis of other Trinity systems in the ancient world, i.e. Hindu: Brahma-Vishnu-Shiva and the Christian Trinity: Father-Son-Holy Ghost.

Lines 33-34 of the Ancient Egyptian Hymn of Amun provides a profound mystical insight into the true meaning of the universal trinity symbol of *Amun-Ra-Ptah.*

> *33. He whose name is hidden is Amun, Ra belongeth to him as His face, and the body is Ptah.*
> *34. Their cities are established on earth forever, Waset, Anu, Hekap-tah.*

Amun, the Self, is the "hidden" essence of all things. The Sun (Ra) is the radiant and dynamic outward appearance of the hidden made manifest and also the light of cosmic consciousness, the cosmic mind or that through which consciousness projects. In this aspect, Ptah represents the physical world, the solidification or coagulation of the projection of consciousness (Amun) made manifest. These manifestations are reproduced symbolically on earth in the cities of *KMT* (Egypt) and Waset (Weset) or Newt(Greek - Thebes). Waset was named Thebes by the Greeks, who knew it also as *Diospolis* ("heavenly city"). Thebes is the city identified in the Old Testament as *No* ("city"), *No-Amon* ("city of Amon"), *Anu* (city of Ra) and *Hekaptah* (city of Ptah).

The Trinity also refers to the three states of consciousness (*waking, Dream and Deep Dreamless Sleep*), the three levels of religion (*Ritual-Mythological-Metaphysical*), the three subtle bodies (*Physical-Astral-Causal*), the three levels of initiatic education (*Mortals-The Intelligences-The Creators or Beings of Light*) and the triune program for studying the mystical teachings prescribed by the ancient Temple of Isis: *Listening, Reflection, Meditation*.

If you have had some experience with the Christian faith you will probably notice some resemblance to the Christian Trinity. This relationship is due to the fact that early Christianity had its roots in ancient Egypt and it adopted many of the ancient Egyptian teachings and renamed them to suit the new generation and the needs of the ancient Roman Empire which controlled it. This theme will be developed in the following lessons since it is important to the deeper understanding of the origins and teachings of Christian Myth and Theology.

Egyptian Physics Through
Memphite Cosmology and Cosmogony

The diagram on the facing page depicts the Company of gods and goddesses of Ptah and the principles which they represent. The opposites of creation emanate from the oneness of the Self.

Neter Neteru, Nebertcher - Amun
(unseen, hidden, ever present, Supreme Being, beyond duality and description)

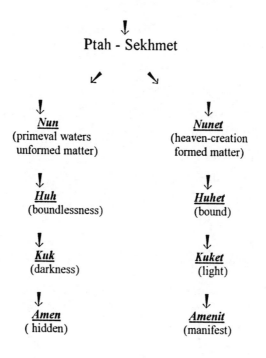

↓
Ptah - Sekhmet

↙ ↘

↓	↓
Nun	**_Nunet_**
(primeval waters unformed matter)	(heaven-creation formed matter)
↓	↓
Huh	**_Huhet_**
(boundlessness)	(bound)
↓	↓
Kuk	**_Kuket_**
(darkness)	(light)
↓	↓
Amen	**_Amenit_**
(hidden)	(manifest)

According to the diagrams on pages 82-83 depicting the process of creation outlined in the Shabaka Inscription, from God emanated matter (neters) and their qualities. Therefore, the world itself is the body of God, who enters (inhabits) the various objects of the world: wood, minerals, clay, etc. Thus, from this teaching it is to be understood that there are no such things as separate objects. God is all that exists. You, the reader, are God, the paper upon which this work is written is also God, the instruments you are using to read (your eyes) are God, and the thoughts used to think and the intellect used to make sense of these writings are also God.

The Mystical *Uas*

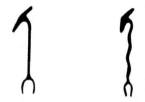

Three of the most important symbols which Ptah is associated with are the *Uas*, *Ankh* and the *Tet*. The *Uas* scepter, 1 , is a symbol of "power" and "dominion" which many of the gods and pharaohs may be seen holding. It is composed of a straight shaft with the head of a mythical animal associated with the God *Set* (Seth), who represents egoism, evil and ignorance as well as raw power and brute strength.

Set is the neter who presides over the egoistic tendencies of the human being. Set is the aspect of the human mind which is ignorant of its true self and as a result develops impulses of selfishness, greed, mischievousness, lust, boastfulness, arrogance, vanity, anger, indulgence in sense pleasures, undisciplined, impulsiveness, rudeness, etc. The definition of the name Set includes *extroverted, emitting nature, pride and insolence.* According to Plutarch, Set is the name of *one who, full of ignorance and error, tears in pieces and conceals that holy doctrine which the goddess* (Isis) *collects, compiles, and delivers to those who aspire after the most perfect participation in divine nature.* Egoism produces ignorance and error which block wisdom and experience of the Divine.

The task of sublimating the ego is embodied in the Egyptian story of the battle between Horus and Set which is a part of the Osirian Resurrection Mystery (see The book *The Ausarian Resurrection: The Ancient Egyptian*

The Ancient Egyptian symbol of The Primeval Ocean

All existence is likened to a vast ocean because the ocean is a single all-encompassing, all-pervasive, essence which accepts all rivers without becoming full and which is the source and sustenance of all life on earth.

In the same way, all matter in the universe is part of one all-encompassing essence from which all of the different forms emerge and take shape and into which they decay and dissolve through the cycle of time.

Bible). In the myth, Set (ego), out of greed, tears to pieces (fragmented) Osiris (the soul), who is the father of Horus. Due to this act, Horus (spiritual aspiration - intuitional vision) engages in a struggle against Set to redeem his father. He must redeem the *Eye*, the center of his power, which Set stole. Set, as the lower self (ego), is in continuous conflict with Horus, who also represents the soul or higher self as an incarnation of his father. After a long conflict, Horus succeeds in controlling Set by reconstructing the damaged *Eye* and controlling Set's sexual energy. When this occurs, Horus becomes the ithyphallic *Amsu-Min* or Horus in the aspect of *overthrower of the enemies of his father.*

After the struggle, Set ends up in the service of the Self (Ra). This is symbolized by the depiction of Set assisting the voyage of the sacred barque of Ra as it traverses the heavens and is attached by fiends (chaos and unrighteousness) who were previously Set's accomplices. Set's energy is transformed from raw sexuality to spiritual ecstasy as it is placed at the service of the Higher Self. Set becomes a champion who fights against the forces of evil (anger, hate, greed, etc.), which in the past, he himself represented. There are several pictures showing that Horus and Set are aspects of the same being. Both represent the conflicting aspects of the human mind. When the lower self (Set) is mastered and placed in the service of the higher (Horus), then spiritual realization is assured. The same idea is conveyed in the *Sphinx*. It represents the embodiment of the initiatic ideal, the infinite energy and life force of nature, symbolized by the animal body, commanded by the intuitive intellect, symbolized by the human head.

The *Uas* or *Was* symbol represents the energy which engenders life. When this energy is controlled by the ignorant ego, evil, negative activity, restlessness, agitation and unrest are the result. When the same energy is sublimated and controlled, divine work can be accomplished in a most effective and exalted manner. Thus, any being who holds the *Was* is in control of the source and power of the Soul. It means having dominion over one's desires and passions, and being free from delusion and ignorance as to one's true nature. In a historical, political or exoteric sense, this implies being the pharaoh who resides in Waset. However, the esoteric symbolism implies that the possessor of the *Uas* is in communion with the Supreme Ruler of *Waset,* who is none other than Amun, the Divine Self. Thus, the Was scepter was the emblem of Waset as well as the the head ornament of the goddess of the city itself, who was also known as *Waset.*

The Mystical Ankh

The Ankh, ♀ , is the symbol of the imper-ishable vital force of life. It is related to the life giving properties of air and water. The Ankh depicts three symbolic principles found in creation: 1. The circle (female member) 2. the cross (male member) and 3. Unity (the male member united with that of the female). Life literally occurs as a result of the union of spirit and matter, the circle representing the immortal and eternal part (absolute reality) and the cross representing that which is mortal and transient (illusion-matter).

Thus, as with the Ying and Yang symbol of the Chinese Tao philosophy, the Ankh also symbolizes the balance between the two forces of life, positive-negative, light-dark, long-short, female-male, etc. If properly balanced and cultivated, the power of harmony (union of opposites) is formidable. The top of the Ankh, the circle, represents the Shen, the Egyptian symbol of eternity. In Indian - Hindu Mythology, the Ankh is depicted in the pictures of the androgynous God-Goddess *Ardhanari.* The left side of Ardhanari is female and the right side is male. In Chinese philosophy, the Shen represents the life force in the cosmos; it is the wisdom-consciousness, the Spirit.

The Ankh is also known as the *"key of life."* To give an Ankh to someone in thought or deed is to wish that person life and health. A most important feature of the Ankh symbol is that it is composed of two separable parts. That is to say, the loop at the top (female) and the cross at the bottom (male) are only "tied" together as it were. Therefore, it is possible to loosen the bonds (knots) that tie the spirit to the body and thus make it possible for the soul to attain enlightenment. Ankh may be pronounced Aung and used as a Hekau (word of power or Mantra), chanting repeatedly (aloud or mentally) while concentrating on the meaning behind the symbolism. Staring at the symbols either alone or in conjunction with the hekau or simply concentrating on it (alone) mentally will help steady the mind during concentration and meditation.

The Mystical Tet

The *Tet* pillar, ▯, is associated with Ptah as well as Osiris. It is part of a profound mystical teaching that encompasses the mystical Life Force energy which engenders the universe and which is the driving force which sustains life and impels human beings to action. In the Ausarian Resurrection myth, it is written that when Osiris was killed by Set, his body was thrown into the Nile and it came ashore on the banks of Syria. There it grew into a tree with a fragrant aroma and the kin of that land had it cut into a pillar. The pillar of Osiris-Ptah refers to the human vertebrae and the Serpent Power or life Force energy which exists in the subtle spine of every human being. It refers to the four highest states of psycho-spiritual consciousness in a human being with the uppermost tier symbolizing enlightenment. Also, the Tet refers to the special realm of the Ṭuat (astral plane) in much the same way as the Christian *Tree of Life* refers to resurrection in Christian mystical mythology.

The Tet refers to a special realm within the Ṭuat or Ancient Egyptian concept of the *Netherworld*. This is the abode of Osiris-Ptah as well as the ultimate destination of those who become enlightened. It is the realm of Supreme Peace. It is known as *Sekhet-Aaru* or in other times *Amentet*. Amentet is a reference which unites the symbolism of Osiris and Ptah with that of Amun because *Tet*, ⬚, refers to the Tet or Djed Pillar of Osiris and Ptah. The Tet symbolizes the awakening human soul who is well "established" or "steadfast" or "stable" in the knowledge of the Self. *Tettetu*, ⬚⬚⬚ ⬚ ⬚, refers to the abode of Osiris.

Tattu was the name of two towns in Ancient Egypt. In mystical terms it refers to being firmly established in the Netherworld. The Ancient Egyptian word *Tattu* refers to "steadfastness" or "stability" as well as the pillar of Osiris. This is the principle being referred to in the following line from the *Egyptian Book of Coming Forth By Day*, Chapter I: 13-15:

𓊖𓏏𓏏𓇋𓏏 𓊃𓏏𓏏𓇋𓏏 ... *(hieroglyphs)*

nuk Tetteti, se Tetteti au am-a em Tettetu

Mesi - a em Tettetu

"I am Tetteti (steadfast), son of Tetteti (steadfast), conceived and born in the region of Tettetu (steadfastness)."

The Ancient Egyptian concept of creation includes three realms. These are the TA, ⟹ 𐏉 (Earth), Pet, ⟞ (Heaven), and the Ṭuat ⋆ 𓃭 (the Underworld). Ṭuat is pronounced with the "Ṭ" sounding as a "D" in much the same way as the "*Tao*" of Taoism is pronounced "*Dao*". The Ṭuat is the abode of the gods, goddesses, spirits and souls. It is the realm where those who are evil or unrighteous are punished, but it is also where the righteous live in happiness. It is the "other world", the spirit realm. The Ṭuat is also known as Amenta since it is the realm of Amen (Amun). The Ṭuat is the realm Ra, as symbolized by the sun, traverses after reaching the western horizon, in other words, the movement of Ra between sunset and sunrise, i.e. at night. Some people thought that the Ṭuat was under the earth since they saw Ra traverse downward and around the earth and emerged in the east, however, this interpretation is the understanding of the uninitiated masses. The esoteric wisdom about the Tuat is that it is the realm of the unconscious human mind and at the same time, the realm of cosmic consciousness or the mind of God. Both the physical universe and the Astral plane, the Tuat, are parts of that cosmic consciousness.

Thus, the mystical reading of the symbolism above shows that Ptah symbolizes the Life Force energy which engenders life within creation. Ptah is the root of all creation.

*(see *The Serpent Power* by Muata Ashby)

PART IIII
The Deeper Implications
of the
Ancient Egyptian
Concept of the
Primeval Ocean

NUN

NU: THE PRIMEVAL OCEAN

Ancient Egyptian Mythology is filled with stories of gods and goddesses, but all of them are related in a harmonious manner, which when understood correctly, helps to unlock the mysteries of the human heart. Ancient Egyptian mythology begins with the existence of the Nu, the Primeval Ocean. The creation stories of the Bible, the Cabala (Jewish Mysticism) and the Upanishads are remarkably similar in the notion of primeval formlessness and in the subsequent names and forms (differentiation and objectification of matter) which arose later.

Ancient Egyptian Shabaka Inscription:

> "Ptah conceived in his heart (reasoning consciousness) all that would exist and at his utterance (the word - will, power to make manifest), created Nun, the primeval waters (unformed matter-energy).

> Then, not having a place to sit, Ptah causes Nun to emerge from the primeval waters as the Primeval Hill so

that he may have a place to sit. Atom (Atum) then emerges and sits upon Ptah. Then came out of the waters four pairs of Gods, the Ogdoad (eight Gods):

From Genesis 1 (Bible):

1. In the beginning God created the heaven and the earth.
2. And the earth was without form, and void; and darkness [was] upon the face of the deep. And the Spirit of God moved upon the face of the waters.

From the Sepher (Sefir) Yezirah (Cabalism):

These are the ten spheres of existence, which came out of nothing. From the spirit of the Living God emanated air, from the air, water, from the water, fire or ether, from the ether, the height and the depth, the East and the West, the North and the South.

From the Zohar (Cabalism):

> Before God manifested Himself, when all things were still hidden in him... He began by forming an imperceptible point; this was His own thought. With this thought He then began to construct a mysterious and holy form...the Universe.

From the Laws of Manu (Indian):

Manu is a Sage-Creator God of Indian Hindu-Vedic tradition who recounts the process of Creation wherein the *Self Existent Spirit* (GOD) felt desire. Wishing to create all things from his own body, GOD created the primeval waters (Nara) and threw a seed into it. From the seed came the golden cosmic egg. The Self Existent Spirit (Narayana) developed in the egg into Brahma (Purusha) and after a year of meditation, divided into two parts (Male and Female).

When we think of our body we don't differentiate between the left leg and the right, the lips and the face, or the fingers and the arm. In a mysterious way, we consider all of the parts as a whole and call this "me". In the same way, in the state of Enlightenment, the entire universe is understood as "me". Consciousness is essentially pure until the association with the ego develops. Then multiplicity and duality appear to exist but as the following passages explain, the multiplicity of creation is merely the forms which energy takes on as it moves and interacts in different polarities or the pairs of opposites. This concept of vibrations being the underlying cause of the phenomenal world existed within the Egyptian mystical text called *The Kybalion:*

"To change your mood or mental state, change your vibration."

"Mastery of self consists not in abnormal dreams, visions and fantastic imaginings or living, but in using the higher forces against the lower thus escaping the pains of the lower by vibrating on the higher."

"Mind, as matter, may be transmuted from state to state, degree to degree, condition to condition, pole to pole and vibration to vibration. Transmutation is a Mental Art."

"To destroy an undesirable rate of mental vibration, concentrate on the opposite vibration to the one to be suppressed."

"The wise ones serve the higher planes and rule the lower, in this way one operates the laws instead being a slave to them."

"Those who may come to understand the law of vibrations will hold the scepter of power in their hand."

"Nothing rests, everything moves; everything vibrates."

"Gender is in everything; everything has its Masculine and Feminine Principles; Gender manifests on all planes."

"Everything is dual; everything has poles; everything has its pair of opposites; like and unlike are the same; opposites are identical in nature, but different in degree;

extremes meet; all truths are but half-truths; all paradoxes may be reconciled."

"Everything flows out and in; everything has its tides; all things rise and fall; the pendulum-swing manifests in everything; the measure of the swing to the right is the measure to the left; rhythm compensates."

"Every cause has its Effect; every Effect has its Cause; everything happens according to Law; Chance is a name for Law unrecognized; there are many planes of causation, but nothing escapes the Law."

The 11 preceding tenets point to some very important teachings about the nature of Creation, the mind and about the way in which the universe exists. First, the physical world appears real because of the senses. The human senses react with physical objects and concludes that they are real, however, as you already know, modern physics has already proven that matter is not solid just as ancient mystical philosophy has taught for thousands of years. So we must conclude that the senses are limited in their capacity to perceive reality the way it truly is. The teachings state that the entire universe and everything in it vibrates. This follows along with the understanding of the Ancient Egyptian creation story which speaks about a Primeval Ocean from which God emerged by uttering his own name. Sounds are vibrations and vibrations ripple through the ocean of Consciousness. However, sounds are nothing more than the gross manifestation of thoughts which are themselves also vibrations. This means that everything in Creation, all objects, are manifestations of vibrations in the ocean consciousness just as every object in your dream is a manifestation of your consciousness which is being rippled, as it were, by your thought vibrations. A deeper reflection on this teaching leads to the understanding that happy as well as sad thoughts are nothing but vibrations in your consciousness. All of your thoughts, life experiences, dreams, desires and aspirations are nothing but vibrations in your consciousness. Your "physical" body is not physical in reality. It is a gross manifestation of your thought vibrations.

Since the mind is essentially energy, that energy can be trained to act or perceive in particular ways. You have the choice of perceiving yourself as a subject living within all of your experiences, which are limited vibrations, or of discovering the deeper source of your existence. According to the texts, most people are incapable of controlling their emotions, moods and feelings because they do not realize that their real Self is separate from these. Emotions, moods and feelings are nothing but vibrations, they are not you. Most people cannot separate themselves from their thoughts or mental complexes or conditioning. This means that their entire existence is in the realm of ignorance wherein they identify themselves with the body and thoughts of the mind as themselves and are unaware of their spiritual Self. This is the process of identification or conditioning. They identify their existence with the experiences and sense perceptions, thus they are unable to discover a deeper reality, the Soul. Identification means that they identify their existence, their life and death, with the experiences, life and death of the body. They believe that this is what they are and nothing more. In reality, the soul is never affected by the vibrations in consciousness. Further, in the same way that you realize that "nothing" happened, in reality, once you wake up from a dream, a Sage understands that from the point of view of the Soul nothing really happens, nothing changes. The varied experiences of life, world history and so forth are only vibrations in the mind. In reality, there is only the calm peace of the ocean and the waves becoming only amusing experiences instead of events which inspire fear, elation, regret, anger, or desire of any kind. When one believes that a mirage is real, one may pursue that mirage, however, when one realizes that it was only an illusion, one should no longer continue to pursue that mirage. Therefore, when a Sage discovers his/ her true identity as the Self, they become fearless of anything that can happen in the phenomenal world just as when one wakes up in a middle of a dream one is not affected by the events of the dream. They are understood as being an illusion, a passing fancy. This is the attitude which a Sage has towards life. When one understands that what one is looking at is a mirage, the mirage appearance may continue, however one will not be fooled. The physical objects of the universe are indeed like a mirage. Though appearing to exist as abiding, solid realities, ancient mystical philosophy as well as modern physics show how in reality they are something other than solid and abiding.

In the Kybalion, the universe is explained as a vibration. Also the mind and the mental substance from which thoughts are made is also composed of vibrations. In the realm described above, where Osiris abides, there is no vibration; "nothing happens" from the point of view of a human being because this realm does not exist as a factor of mentation. Think about it. Everything you know or have experienced in your life has been a factor of your thinking process. In fact, without this thinking process the mind cannot function; it will stand still. When the mind operates, it vibrates, and this vibration stirs up the ocean of consciousness. This stirring or vibratory process is what people perceive as life experiences, sense perceptions, awareness of the passage of time, awareness of space between objects and their thoughts. Upon closer reflection you should realize that throughout all of your experiences, being born, growing to adulthood, middle age and the aging process, you have been the same all the time. It has always been the same "you" but the experiences are different. Likewise, the experiences of your waking life are not different from those of your dreams. They are all just vibrations in the mental pool of water which is a fraction of the vast ocean of consciousness.

Thus, all experiences occur either in the Tuat (Astral plane composed of the mind and subtle senses) or in the Physical world (the mind, senses and body), which is a creation of the mind of God (The Self) in which the mind and senses of the individual human being interact. Once again, this interaction process in which you see yourself as an individual having experiences in time and space is composed of the Triad (referring to the Trinity). The Triad of consciousness is composed of three aspects. There are objects, a subject and there is interaction between the two. As a soul you are a special reflection of the light of Supreme Consciousness which emanates from the Self (Osiris). This is why you have consciousness and awareness of being alive. However, due to your ignorance you are wandering in the vast realm of the mind which can only operate in the Tuat or in the physical world. You have forgotten your Higher Self which is needed in order to perceive that which transcends the vibrations of the mind and senses.

Also, human emotions and desires such as falling in love or desiring to possess an object in order to experience pleasure all occur in the mind and are in reality projections in the mind based on the persons understanding of reality, just as an entire world is created in a dream out of one's consciousness. Those people and objects which you desired are composed of mental substance and your body and thoughts are also composed of the same substance. Everything is composed of atoms, and atoms are composed of energy, and energy is composed of the Self. In reality, that which you desire is a reflection of God in the mental pool of consciousness (your mind), but through the deluded state of mind one comes to believe that personalities and physical objects in the world are abiding realities. Just as the dream world appears to be "real" and "tangible" during the dream, the physical world also appears to be real and tangible and yet they are composed of the same stuff. In reality the only truth behind all things in creation is the Self and it is this Self which supports all of the vibrations in all planes of existence. Thus, if you desire an object in the world or a person you are in reality desiring the Self. Therefore, the mystics and Sages who have discovered the Self have enjoined the practice of dispassion and detachment. This discipline involves living life but not holding on to it. It is a dynamic quality which, when developed, allows you to experience life while not being bound to it or affected by it. Since both good situations and bad situations in life are both illusory, then it follows that positive developments in life should not become the cause of elation while at the same time negative developments should not be viewed as a motive for depression and sorrow. All situations, good or bad, are determined by the concept of the person who is experiencing them and they are therefore dependent on their attitude or frame of mind. For those who have discovered the reality beyond the illusoriness of the mind and time and space, there is neither good nor bad, happy or sad, only the knowledge of peace and immortality. From the standpoint of those who are unenlightened, all events which occur in life seem real, but from the standpoint of one who has discovered the absolute reality, all of this is illusory as a passing cloud or a dream. Thus, any experience which depends on the mind and senses occurs either in the astral or in the physical plane, and therefore these planes are also illusory and unreal.

When the mind and senses are transcended through the process of meditation it is possible to discover that special realm wherein there is no vibration, no time, no space; there is neither existence nor non-existence, neither being nor non-being. It is the realm that is beyond all concepts of the mind, and it is the realm from which time and space emanates.

All of the states of consciousness which are experienced through the mind (waking, dream and dreamless deep sleep) are nothing but vibrations in consciousness. These states of consciousness are expressions of the Triad of consciousness. They are not real in themselves but they reflect the absolute reality which transcends them. They can exist only because consciousness, the Self, is there to support them just as an image is supported in a mirror because the mirror is present. All vibrations in the mind are like waves in an ocean, in this case, the ocean of consciousness. The ocean supports the waves and these cannot exist separate from the ocean. Also, the thought waves in the mind cannot encompass the entire ocean, therefore, only a portion of consciousness is reflected at any time. This limited reality is what most people are aware of and call life. The experiences of the past, present, future, the awareness of being born, growing up and death are also vibrations in consciousness. Also, your awareness of your history, your memories, your family relationships, etc., are nothing more than vibrations in your mind which is supported by your deeper consciousness, your true Self. They are not really "happening" to the deeper "you". Therefore, life and the phenomenal universe is compared to a "dream" in which various experiences seem to occur but upon waking up, the experiences are discovered to be "unreal" even though while at the time they were happening they seemed to be very real. Thus, the human concept of "time" is only a minute segment along the stream of eternity. The concept of the world as a dream is expressed in the Ancient Egyptian hieroglyphic text entitled: *The Songs of The Harper.* In one verse the relativity of the passage of time and the experiences of life are explained as follows:

"The whole period of things done
on the earth
is but a period of a dream."

The practices of yoga allow the practitioner to discover a deeper reality beyond the mental vibrations. Mental vibrations and identification with them as the Self is due to desire and ignorance. Your desires lead you to have vibrations in your mind. These thought vibrations are related to the object of your desires. Therefore, if you desire worldly experiences you will have thoughts related to those kinds of worldly experiences. But if you desire to discover your true Self, then you will enter a road which will at first lead you to have thoughts about the transcendental reality, but eventually you will be led to a state which is beyond all vibrations. When this state is experienced there is a perception of all-encompassing-ness because the mind and senses are not used. There is calm in the ocean of consciousness because the vibrating waves have subsided.

In this way it must be understood that all vibrations or experiences of the mind are illusory because they are only partial reflections of the Divine. Also, the vibrations in consciousness cannot exist separate from consciousness which perceives them and supports. Objects are essentially vibrating consciousness and the perception of them in the mind of the individual is also due to Consciousness through which the individual operates the senses and interacts with the objects. Therefore, the experiences of the mind are of limitation and the belief in them as "real" and abiding is based on ignorance of the deeper reality. You desire objects because you believe them to be real, however, your desire, the objects, your fanciful notions and longings about them are all in the realm of ignorance. Thus, it must be clearly understood that the experiences of the mind are illusory vibrations and that in order to experience absolute reality it is necessary to transcend all vibrations in the relative states of ordinary human consciousness (waking, dream and dreamless deep sleep). This can be accomplished through the practices of yoga. When you begin to understand the illusoriness of physical objects and the ignorance of your desire for them, the pressure of your *Karma* or the beliefs, desires, longings and ignorance about reality, which impels you, subsides. This feeling leads you to experience dispassion for the objects of the world, allowing you to begin to discover a new peace and a deeper root to your existence beyond the mind, senses and physical body. When this root begins to be discovered by you, you are treading the path of knowledge and wisdom.

This teaching about the vibrations also translates into the experience of duality. When there is calm in the ocean of consciousness, there is the experience of oneness, singularity. When there are many waves, however, then there is the perception of the one plus others or duality and multiplicity. However, the one and the others are in reality supported by the same source. When the vibrating waves subside, they melt back into the ocean of oneness. Therefore, oneness is the deeper reality behind duality since duality is in reality a manifestation of the oneness. So all physical objects and living beings are in reality rooted to the deeper oneness and source of all creation even though they appear to be separate and distinct from each other just as the myriad of thoughts in the mind are in reality surges in the ocean of consciousness that subside into Consciousness.

From the Kabbalah:

Polarity is the principle that runs through the whole of Creation, and is in fact, the basis of manifestation. Polarity really means the flowing of force from a sphere of high pressure to a sphere of low pressure; high and low being always relative terms. Every sphere of energy needs to receive the stimulus of an influx of energy at higher pressure, and to have an output into a sphere of lower pressure. The source of all energy is the Great Unmanifest (God), and it makes its own way down the levels, changing its form from one to the other, till it is finally "earthed" in matter.

The pure impulse of dynamic creation is formless; and being formless, the creation it gives rise to can assume any and every form.

The following passage comes from *Lao-Tzu*, the classical Taoist writer who popularized Taoism in China at the same time that *Buddha* and *Mahavira* developed Buddhism and Jainism in India. He further illustrates the idea of undifferentiated versus differentiated consciousness.

There was something undifferentiated and yet complete, which existed before heaven and earth. Soundless and formless, it depends on nothing and does not change.

It operates everywhere and is free
from danger.
It may be considered the mother of
the universe.

The same idea of *"formlessness"* or
"undifferentiated" matter occurs in the *Rig*
(Rik) *Veda*, the Upanishads and the Bhagavad
Gita from India as well. The same teaching of
"vibrations" which was presented above in the
Kybalion is also present in the teachings of the
Upanishads and is referred to as *Spanda* or
vibrations. The only difference between the
following texts is that the Gita applies all of the
attributes of the manifest and unmanifest nature
of divinity and incorporates them in the anthro-
pomorphic personality of Krishna.

From the Rig Veda:

There was neither non-existence
nor existence then; there was neither the realm of space nor the the
sky beyond.
There was no distinguishing sign
of night nor of day...
Desire came upon that one in the

beginning; that was the first seed of mind.

From the Upanishads:

There are, assuredly, two forms of the Eternal: the formed and the formless, the mortal and the immortal, the stationary and the moving, the actual and the yon.

Gita: Chapter 9:17

Lord Krishna: I am the Father of the universe; I am the Mother, the sustainer, as well as the Grandfather. I am the goal of Vedic knowledge, I am the sacred Om, I am verily the Vedas in the form of Rik, Yaju and Sama.

Insights Into The Ancient Egyptian Primordial Ocean

Before there was any god or goddess, even Ra or Osiris and Isis, and before there was any physical matter, the planets, the sun, animals, human beings, etc., there was the Primeval

Ocean and from it emanated all that exists. There are stories of a Primeval Ocean in other cultures. Hinduism also includes teachings in reference to the Primeval Ocean and the Christian Bible begins with creation out of primeval waters in the book of Genesis. The oldest notion and greatest emphasis on the concept of the Primeval Ocean comes from Ancient Egypt.

In the same manner that waves arise out of the sea and appear to be formed of different shapes, sizes and textures, the objects of the phenomenal universe, the sun, stars, planets trees, animals and all living beings arise out of this ocean. But this rising did not only occur once in the "beginning of time". It is continually occurring. All objects in nature are continuously sustained by an "unseen" force which modern science cannot fully explain. However, science does explain some characteristics of the phenomenal universe and these reveal an ocean of energy wherein all things are interrelated and bound together as opposed to the ordinary thinking of a universe full of separate objects which are composed of different elements. In fact, modern science reveals that all objects in the universe are composed of the same "stuff". All of the "elements" have the same basis, energy. Further, all matter is merely a manifestation of that same essence but in different modes of manifestation. This facet of matter was explained thousands of years ago by the sages of mystical wisdom.

The sages have shown that consciousness or pure awareness is the basis of all matter just as when you are not thinking, there are no thoughts or vibrations in the consciousness of your mind. In the same way, this universe is a manifestation of the thought process of the Supreme Being. Therefore, it is possible to have an infinite number of elements and combinations of those elements just as it is possible for you to create anything in your mind, out of your consciousness, when applied towards the imaginative process.

When the body dies it returns to the earth from whence it arose. Where does the soul go? It returns to the ocean of consciousness, and if it is not enlightened, returns to this physical plane of existence to have more human experiences. When enlightenment is attained through the practice of yoga, one communes with the ocean of pure and infinite consciousness which is an ever existing reality beyond the grasp of those who are devoid of spiritual sensitivity. Our limited minds are like waves in the ocean of the Supreme Being. However, though they seem to be separate and we seem to be alone, in reality, God is always there and is the very fabric of all physical objects as well as the very source and sustenance of human consciousness. It is due to the distractions of the mind caused by desires, illusions, cravings, longings and ignorance that the innermost recesses of our unconscious mind is veiled from conscious awareness. Nevertheless, the exterior world and the internal world are nothing but manifestations of the primeval waters, manifestations of God or the Self.

When we delve deeply into the mysteries of the ocean of consciousness within our minds, we are able to discover the deeper truths about our real essence, origin and purpose. This is the process called *Sheti*. When the wisdom teachings are studied deeply and the mystical implications are understood, a special form of transformation occurs which leads to the discovery of the highest spiritual truths within one's heart. Discovering this glorious truth of your true nature is the goal of yoga and all mystical philosophies.

Thus, in the same way as a form is within a stone and can be carved into a sculpture, all objects in creation exist, arise and dissolve into the Primeval Ocean. In other words, from the singular, preexistent ocean of consciousness arises all that exists as a thought in the mind of God in the form of a Trinity or Triad of consciousness. Therefore, from the one arises the three.

The Self, God, is a sea of pure consciousness (NUNU or NUN), and out of that same sea came creation. Creation then is the sea which has been rippled with waves by the wind of thought vibrations. These thought vibrations are the result of desire. In the same way a placid lake reflects the unbroken image of the moon and when disturbed by a rock develops ripples, the pure consciousness of the mind is fragmented and rippled, as it were, by the thought waves caused by desire for worldly experiences. Because of this rippling of consciousness, there appear to be many moons when there is in reality only one. If the lake of the mind were to be calmed, if there were no desires, then the mind would reflect its essential unity and non-duality. The primeval waters never changed into creation. Creation is the primeval waters itself and is continuously changing according to the winds of Cosmic vibration as prescribed by the Cosmic Mind (God). Therefore, Creation is a continuous process which occurs every moment by God's consciousness, i.e. God's very presence.

All matter is in reality cosmic mental thought substances in varying degrees of vibration and varying degrees of subtlety. The subtlest material is the Self, God, and the Self permeates all other things from the less subtle material which composes the Astral world (Ṭuat) to the grosser material which composes the physical world. All matter is in a state of vibration and its existence is continually being sustained by the Self. This process of sustaining Creation occurs every instant of every day, just as the form and structure of the human body is sustained by a continuous process of new cells being created to substitute for those which are dying off. Every cell in the body is changed every year. Therefore, you do not have the same body you had a year ago. In the same way the atoms of the house you live in are not the same as they were in the past, even though the house "looks" to be the same as before. This is why what is considered to be "solid" matter is not solid at all, and it is also the reason why things break down. There is no object which escapes the power of time which withers away everything. Sooner or later everything breaks down and dissolves back into its original state. Even the most spectacular monuments and architectural creations will someday deteriorate to the point of no longer being usable. Look at the Pyramids and the Sphinx. Having withstood the ravages of time for over 12,000 years they are showing signs of deterioration. Even the most perfectly constructed machine or object cannot escape the movement of time.

Think of a building. What is its life span? Say that it will last one hundred years and then will have to be torn down to build a new one. Every year there is a certain amount of destruction or dissolution which occurs in the atoms of the building. It could be said that it breaks down one hundredth of its life span every year. The movement of dissolution is slow and those who do not reflect on it do not acknowledge the hidden mystical teaching until the time of the dissolution of their own body; then it is too late. You must study and understand the teachings of mystical spirituality now while there is "time".

Another important teaching to understand about "matter" is that the substratum of all objects is the same, and therefore, all objects can be transmuted or transformed into others. Even the most foul smelling rotten matter can be rearranged at the molecular or subatomic level and changed into the most fragrant sub-stance. Solid matter can be converted into energy and then back into solid material form once again. These findings have been confirmed by modern physics experiments.

The underlying power of time comes from the continuous process of movement in Creation. In the same manner that the human mind does not "stand still", the universe is in continuous motion. Even at subatomic levels, matter, regardless of how solid it may appear to be, changes. The physical universe is in constant dissolution and creation. This is the reason why the solar and lunar barque of Amun-Ra (𓊪𓏏)

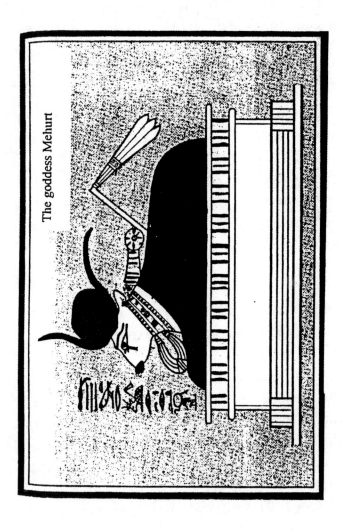

The goddess Mehurt

traverses the heavens perpetually and must constantly battle the forces of chaos and disorder (Set). Amun-Ra constantly establishes Maat (cosmic order) and thereby maintains the phenomenal universe in existence. The barque traverses through the heavens and every evening is consumed by the Cow-Goddess, Nut, and every morning she gives birth to it with renewed life.

The Pyramid texts of *Pepi II* determine the Company of gods and goddesses of Anu to be: Tem, Shu, Tefnut, Geb, Nut, Osiris, Isis, Set and Nephthys. In the pyramid texts of *Pepi II*, the following account is given about the emergence of Atum (or Tem, Tum):

> He who was born in the Nu (primeval waters),
> before the sky came into being,
> before the earth came into being,
> before the two supports* came into being,
> before the quarrel** took place,
> before that fear which arose on account of the
> Eye of Horus existed...
>   *(Shu-Tefnut)
> **(quarrel between Horus and Set)

The idea of the primeval waters (NU) and the original primeval spirit which engendered life in it occurs in several myths. The earliest occurrence of the idea of the primeval waters is found in the Egyptian religion which predates the Osirian Resurrection Myth. This pre-dynastic (10000-5500 B.C.E.), pre-Osirian, myth spoke of a God who was unborn and undying, and who was the origin of all things. This deity was un-namable, unfathomable, transcendental, gender-less and without form, although encompassing all forms. This being was the God of Light which illumines all things and thus was later associated (in dynastic times) with the Sun, *Ra* or *Tem*, and with *Horus* who represents *that which is up there*. Tum, Tem or Temu is an ancient Egyptian name for the female ocean, the deep and boundless abyss of consciousness from which the phenomenal universe was born. Tum comes from the root *tem*, "to be complete", or *temem*, which means "to make an end of". Also Tum is regarded as the evening or setting sun in the western sky symbolizing the completion, the end, of the journey. *Khepera (or Khepri)*, the dung beetle, represents the morning sun which is becoming. This form is also associated with the young Horus, *Horus in the Horizon,* also known as *The Sphinx.* Ra ☉ represents the daytime sun which *is.* This is why the initiate wishes to go to the *beautiful west* upon completion of the span of life. The beautiful west is the abode of Osiris. Tum was analogous in nature to the Babylonian *Tiamat,* the Chaldean *Thamte,* the Hebrew *Tehorn,* and the Greek *Themis.*

 Ra

The story related in the Papyrus of Nesi-Amsu is that this primeval God laid an egg in the primeval chaotic waters from which the God (Him/Herself) emerged. While this primordial God, who emerged out of the waters, created or emanated Ra, the Sun or Life Force, Tehuti, the Word or creative medium, and MAAT, the principle of cosmic order and regularity, the underlying emphasis was on all of these, as well as human beings and the phenomenal world, being essentially emanations from that same primeval ocean. Other stories tell of how the creator masturbated and engendered life within *Himself.* The papyrus of Nesi-Amsu further discusses the emergence:

When Atum emerged
from Nun, the pri-
mordial waters, be-
fore the sky and earth
were born and before
the creation of worm
or reptile, he found
no place to stand...

Tum, therefore represents the first emerging thought which contemplated its own existence in the vast ocean of undifferentiated consciousness which was devoid of names and forms, devoid of tangibleness, solidification, coagulation and grossness.* All that existed was subtle matter, the primeval ocean. The pyramid texts continue, explaining how Atum continued the process of creation by emitting the other principles of creation in the form of the gods and goddesses as follows. (*capable of being touched; material; something palpable or concrete)

"Tum (Atum) is he who came into
being (through Himself) in Anu.
He took His phallus in His grasp
that he might create joy in Himself, emitting the twins Shu (air,

132

dryness, space, ether) and Tefnut (moistness)..."

In this manner, the various qualities of matter emanated from Tum and gave form to the primeval ocean, and continue to give it form at every moment. Geb is the son of Shu and Tefnut and represents the solid earth. Nut is the daughter of Shu and Tefnut and represents the sky and the heavens and the mother of Osiris, Isis, Set and Nephthys.

In a creation story involving Khepera (Ra in the aspect of the rising sun, the creation of a new day), He says He rose up from Nu and:

"I found no place there whereon I could stand. I worked a charm upon my heart, I laid a foundation in Maa*, and then I made every form. I was one by myself, {since} I had not yet emitted from myself the god Shu, and I had not spit out from myself the goddess Tefnut; there was no other being who worked with me." (*referring to MAAT)

In the creation story involving the Osirian Mysteries, Osiris assumes the role of Khepera and Tem:

> "Neb-er-tcher saith, I am the creator of what hath come into being, and I myself came into being under the form of the god Khepera, and I came into being in primeval time. I had union with my hand, and I embraced my shadow in a love embrace; I poured seed into my own mouth, and I sent forth from myself issue in the form of the gods Shu and Tefnut." "I came into being in the form of Khepera, and I was the creator of what came into being, I formed myself out of the primeval matter, and I formed myself in the primeval matter. My name is Ausares (Osiris).
>
> I was alone, for the gods and goddesses were not yet born, and I had emitted from myself neither Shu nor Tefnut. I brought into my own mouth, *hekau*, and I forthwith

came into being under the form of things which were created under the form of Khepera".

Neb-er-tcher

These passages all point to the fact that while the name of the Supreme Being has changed under the different priesthoods, these are merely different expressions of the same principles and teachings which even use the same wording, therefore, there is no discontinuity or confusion within the theology. More importantly, the last passage reminds us that all of the names and forms are merely outward expressions of the Supreme Being, *Neb-er-tcher*, in its physical manifestation. Nebertcher, as previously discussed, is a name which signifies the all-encompassing meaning of the collective members of the Trinity. Nebertcher includes all male and female aspects of the Trinity and is therefore, to be understood as the androgynous and primordial being from which arose all names and forms, all gods and goddesses, all creation.

These utterances are the progenitors of the Christian and Hebrew idea of creation described in the book of Genesis where God or the Spirit hovers over and stirs the primeval waters. The original Bible texts express the creation more in terms of an act of sexual union. *Elohim* (Ancient Hebrew for Gods/Goddesses) impregnates the primeval waters with *ruach,* a Hebrew word which means *spirit, wind* or the verb *to hover*. The same word means *to brood* in Syriac. Thus, as the book of Genesis explains, creation began as the spirit of God moved over the waters and agitated those waters into a state of movement. In Western traditions, the active role of divinity has been assigned to the male gender while the passive (receiving) role has been assigned to the female gender. This movement constitutes the dynamic *female* aspect of the Divine in Tantric (Eastern and African) terms while the potential-passive aspect is male. Creation is therefore understood to be a product of the interaction between these two aspects of the same reality: spirit and primeval waters (Male and Female).

Since God is all that exists, then God is also the spirit and the primeval waters at the same time. Therefore, God interacts with him/herself and emanates creation out of him/herself. So within this teaching of the Primeval Waters in the Bible lies the mystical idea that creation and God are one and the same in a mysterious unexplained way. Some important questions arise here. If the Spirit is God and the Primeval Waters of Creation are also God then what is Creation and where is the *Kingdom of Heaven?* Is creation separate from God, or is Creation held in the palm of Gods hand? Does God have hands? Where is God? Where did God come from? What is our relation to God?, and so forth. What does this all mean? The study of Ancient Egyptian and Indian creation stories provides answers to these questions.

The Ancient Egyptian and Hindu creation stories originated in the far reaches of antiquity (5500 BCE and 3000 BCE respectively). The primeval Egyptian creation myth is similar in many respects to the creation story from the Indian mythology associated with the *Laws of Manu*. Manu is a Sage-Creator God of Indian Hindu-Vedic tradition who recounts the process of Creation wherein the *Self Existent Spirit* (GOD) felt desire. Wishing to create all things from his own body, GOD created the primeval waters (Nara) and threw a seed into it. From the seed came the golden cosmic egg. The Self Existent Spirit (Narayana) developed in the egg into Brahma (Purusha) and after a year of meditation, divided into two parts (Male and Female). In the Bhagavad Gita, Lord Krishna reiterates the wisdom of the primeval waters as he proclaims that He is the same Supreme Being who arose and formed creation:

> 27. Among the horses know Me
> to be Uchhaihshrava that arose
> during the churning of the ocean; I
> am Airavata among the elephants,
> and the King among human be-
> ings.

Bhagavad Gita: Chapter 10
Vibhuti Yogah--The Yoga of Divine Glories

The teaching of the Primeval Ocean points to another mystical implication. The mind is like an ocean of consciousness, which is being buffeted by the winds of thoughts which have their origin in the ignorance of its true nature and the resulting feelings of greed, hatred, anger, fear, attachment, elation, sorrow and impatience, which are constantly blowing across its surface, creating waves of agitation and distractions in the mind. If these waves were to be calmed, if it were possible to make the mind free of the waves, it would be possible to have clear insight into the depths of one's consciousness just as it would be possible to see the bottom of a lake if it were free of waves. A most important task of every spiritual aspirant is to train the mind so that it is not affected by the winds of emotion and thoughts based on ignorance. When this practice is perfected, there is equanimity in the mind. This equanimity allows you to discover the depths of the ocean of the mind and thus discover the Self within. In order to practice this teaching it is necessary to have a keen understanding of the mystical nature of the universe and of one's own being. Then it is necessary that you live your life according to these teachings and remain mindful of every thought and emotion that enters the mind, rejecting those which are contrary to Maat (order, righteousness, truth) and accepting those that are in line with Maat.

From a Yogic perspective, when you act with reason and uphold justice, correctness and

AMUN-RA-PTAH

PLANES OF EXISTENCE

PA NETER
("The Supreme Divinity)

●

Source of all souls, gods, objects in creation.
Plane of non-duality, no time or space, no separation, all is one.
Realm of mystical experience.

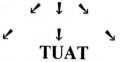

- -

HEAVEN - RA

Causal plane, first realm of duality, refraction of the self, egos develop here. From here down there is Duality and the Triad of perception.

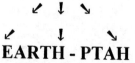

TUAT

Astral plane, composed of mind and subconscious mind (desires, complexes, social conditioning astral body, and emotions. Psychic level.

EARTH - PTAH

Physical plane, physical body and physical objects in time and space.

virtue in your life, you are living according to
Maat and when you live in harmony with Maat
it means that you are moving into harmony with
the universe, God. When you live according to
the whims, desires and feelings of the mind
which are based on ignorance, anger, greed,
fear, hatred and so on, you are living according
to chaos and mental agitation. This is known as
a hellish existence. Therefore, you must strive
to cultivate peace, harmony and love toward
humanity and the universe within your heart.
These qualities will lead you to discover and
experience the deeper essence of your being
just as a swimmer dives below the waves and
discovers the depths of the ocean. In the same
way, you can dive below the waves of mental
agitation (ignorance, anger, greed, fear, hatred,
etc.) and discover the ocean-like Divine Self
within you.

Perhaps the most important teaching to be
derived from the Primeval Ocean is in reference
to its fullness. As a metaphor for consciousness
which holds within itself infinite possibilities
for expression as the universe, the Primeval
Ocean is said to be "Full". This "Fullness"
implies that it is complete, in much the same

way as you are complete as entire dream worlds arise from your mind during sleep. The dream world is apparently "full" also. It seems to contain all of the necessary elements of a "real" world wherein there are people, objects, situations and you as a subject who assumes various identities. Nevertheless, you are the real support of your dream. Its basis lies within your consciousness. In the same way, this entire universe lies within the consciousness of God and God is the substratum of this entire creation just as you are the substratum of your dreams. This teaching of the fullness of the Primeval Ocean is to be found in the *Book of Coming Forth By Day* (xvii. 76,79; lxxi. 13; cxxiv. 17). The hekau-utterance in Chapter xvii gives an exact description of this concept. The initiate says:

"Behold Ra who was born yesterday from the buttocks of the Goddess Mehurt," In the answer to the question: "What then is this?" it is explained: "It is the watery abyss of heaven, or as others say, it is the image of the Eye of Ra in the morning at his daily birth. Mehurt is the Eye (Utchat) of Ra."

Mehurt was originally the female embodiment of the watery matter, the Primeval Ocean from which the substance of the world was formed. Her name ⎯𓏲𓏏𓇳𓄿⎯, means **"mighty fullness"**. She was the infinite source of matter which was impregnated by the male spirit. This is one of the reasons why one of the symbols of Amun is a pregnant woman 𓀎 . Of course, the female primeval matter and the male spirit are both aspects of the same energy. This is expressed in the last line of the utterance where it is explained that Mehurt herself is the "image" of the "Eye of Ra". The Eye of Ra is his own daughter, Hathor, and it is also related to Isis. Mehurt is depicted as a cow goddess brimming with life giving essence. This symbol is common to Hathor, Nut and Isis as well. The cow Goddess is often referred to as a "seven fold deity" known as the "seven Hathors". This title refers to the further differentiation of the three primordial principles which in turn express as the phenomenal universe through a series of sevens. This number seven is expressed in all levels of Creation. It is expressed in the seven levels of the human subtle anatomy with the seven spiritual centers (see Egyptian Yoga) and it is also expressed as

At left: The ancient Egyptian god Ptah-Osiris depicting the same four tiered vertebrae symbol referring to the four upper psycho-spiritual energy centers.

Note the same four tiers on the Uas scepter he is holding.

Below: A three dimensional drawing representing Creation. The four tiers of the Tet refer to states of psycho-spiritual consciousness as well as the nature of the universe. Thus, Ptah is the origin and sustainer of Creation.

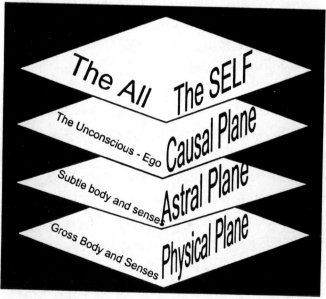

the seven primary colors of the rainbow. This principle of sevens, translated into the Gnostic Idea of the "seven planetary spirits" and the Archangels, known as the heads of the Celestial Host, were titled the "Seven Archangels of the Presence". Isis-Hathor in Ancient Egypt symbolized the source of Creation. The *Milky Way* was produced by her udder and she was "the Great Cow which gave birth to Ra, the Great Goddess, the mother of all the gods and goddesses...the lady who existed when nothing else had being as yet and who created that which came into being."

In Indian Mythology the cow holds the same symbolism as that of Ancient Egypt. The cow is known as the "fountain of milk and curds." In a mystical sense the world is also a curd of the milk which emanated from the celestial cow. To this day the cow is held to be sacred in India and it is associated with Purusha or the Supreme Self in the Avatara personality of Krishna, who is know as the "milker of the cow". Krishna is an incarnation of Vishnu (God) in the same way that Horus (Heru) of Ancient Egypt is an incarnation of Osiris (God). One of Krishna's titles is "Govinda". Govinda

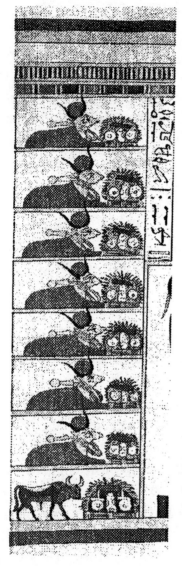

Left: The Seven Hathors (seven celestial cows) and the Bull of Heaven (Osiris) who provide sustenance to the initiate.

Mystically, Osiris-Ptah is the spirit which manifests as creation through the seven levels of energy-consciousness.

From the Papyrus of Ani

Nut consuming the evening sun and giving birth to the morning sun.

means "Cow finder, milker, herder". In a symbolic sense, Krishna is the milker of the Upanishads. He extracts the essence of their wisdom teachings and this essence is presented in the *Bhagavad Gita* text. The Sansktit word "go" (cow) also means "sacred treasure", variously known as the "Philosopher's Stone". The Upanishads are the sacred mystical wisdom texts which expound the teachings of mystical philosophy in much the same way as the "Metu Neter" or Hieroglyphic texts of Ancient Egypt. They are known as "divine speech" or the "words of God" and remarkably, the definition of Metu Neter is also "divine speech" or the "words of God". These similarities point to the essential synchronicity of Ancient Egyptian and modern Indian mystical philosophy.

The Eye of Ra (𓁷) is Ra's creative principle in this aspect. Thus, Creation itself is an image of God. The primordial essence from which Creation arises and that which arises as Creation are images of God, in much the same way as your thoughts and dreams are an image of your consciousness.

𓊡 ⬭ 〰 𓃭𓄿𓇋𓏏𓂝 ⬭ 𓊡

"I was One and then I became
Three"

Through the interplay of the male and female principles an infinite variety of forms can
arise. This is the cause of the multiplicity that is
seen in Creation. The multiplicity of chemical
elements and the infinite possibilities which are
possible through their combinations is in reality
an expression of the two principles, the opposites, duality, which are expressions of the one,
singular and non-dual essence. All of the multiplicity is in reality an expression of the two
principles (duality) which, when examined
closely with keen philosophical reason and an
intuitive mind, is found to be in reality a singular or non-dual principle. This is the deeper
meaning of the Ancient Egyptian teaching: *I
became from God one, Gods three,* which was
presented earlier, where God tells us he was
one essence and then transformed himself into
three. These three constitute the basis of the
multiplicity of creation, the duality along with
the interaction between the two makes three
principles. Thus, the substratum of all creation
is oneness and this oneness has been translated
into religion as the concept of monotheism and

the Trinity. However, monotheism as it is understood in Western religions such as Orthodox Christianity, Orthodox Islam, Orthodox Judaism and others is not the same monotheism implied in the teachings of yoga, and mystical religions such as the Egyptian Mysteries, Vedanta, Buddhism, the Tao, etc.

In Western religion, monotheism implies that there is one God who exists in fact and is watching over his creation. God is conceptualized as a male figure who is separate from creation and manages it from afar. In the mystical sciences, monotheism implies that God is the only being that truly exists and therefore all that exists is an expression of the Divine. Therefore, in mystical philosophy there is no conflict or contradiction with monotheism or polytheism. There is only an expanded definition. In mystical philosophy *Pantheism, Panentheism* and *Monism* are terms which more closely express the understanding of the Divine. The following definitions are presented for the purpose of clarifying the philosophical views held by religion and mystical philosophy.

Polytheism

Polytheism, belief in or worship of many gods. Such gods usually have specific attributes or functions.

Pantheism

1- Absolute Pantheism: Everything there is, is God.
2- Modified Pantheism: God is the reality or principle behind nature.

Panentheism

Term coined by K.C. F. Krause (1781-1832) to describe the doctrine that God is immanent in all things but also transcendent, so that every part of the universe has its existence in God; but He is more than the sum total of the parts.

Shetaut Neter: Ancient Egyptian Religion - Egyptian Yoga

Monotheistic Polytheism - Ancient Egyptian religion encompasses a single and absolute Supreme Deity which expresses as a cosmic forces (gods and goddesses), human beings and nature.

Monism

1- Absolute Monism: Only God is reality. All else is imagination.
2- Modified Monism: God is to nature as soul is to body.

God expresses as nature, the stars, your body, your thoughts, your senses, all physical objects, all good and evil people, etc. God is everything, just as everything in your dreams is in reality an expression of your own consciousness when you sleep. God is not separate from creation but is immanent in creation. God is never far from you but is as close as your every thought, every breath, every sensation, every feeling. Thus, that which transcends the phenomenal world of time and space is "full" and the phenomenal world which is an expression of the eternal is also "full". This exact teaching of the "fullness" of God and the "fullness" of Creation may also be found in the Indian Upanishads in the following prayer:

Purnamadah Purnamidam Purnat
Purnamudachyate Purnasya
Purnamadaya Purnamevavahisyate.
Om Shantih, Shantih, Shantih.*

Translation:

That (Absolute) is full,
this (world, being a manifestation of the Absolute) is full.
When this (world-process) is taken away

(by transcending it through Self-realization), what remains is Full (the Absolute).
May there be Peace, Peace, Peace.*

*From Mantra, Kirtana, Yantra and Tantra
by Sri Swami Jyotirmayananda.

A striking example of the integration of the female principle into Egyptian mythology is to be found in Chapter 78, Line 47 of the Egyptian *Book of Coming Forth By Day* where it is stated to the initiate:

"...To the son (initiate), the Gods have given the crown of millions of years, and for millions of years it allows him to live in the Eye (Eye of Horus), which is the single eye of GOD who is called Nebertcher, the queen of the Gods."

The previous passage is of paramount significance since it states that the primary Trinity, **Nebertcher,** the High GOD of Egypt, which is elsewhere primarily associated with male names, **Amun-Ra-Ptah,** is also *"the queen of the Gods."* Therefore, the primary *"Godhead"* or *Supreme Being* is both **male and female.**

Even in dynastic times the goddess is attributed equal status and importance for the salvation of humanity. All high deities were considered to be bisexual or androgynous, possessing a male and female aspect.

In the Hymns of Amun by *Her* and *Suti*, Amun is called *Glorious Mother of gods and men"*. Thus, either the male or the female aspect or the androgynous aspect of the Divine is emphasized according to the particular idea being expressed. Since the Divine encompasses all genders and that which transcends genders, there is no conflict in any of these interpretations. The conflict in theological study arises when the mental concept of God is concretized and held onto steadfastly as an absolute reality or when it is held on to as being a historical fact rather than a psychological symbol of a deeper reality which is within the human heart and which is also the essence of the universe. This has the effect of stunting spiritual development because eventually, on the way to enlightenment, all concepts must be left behind. Concepts are necessary for the formulation of theories and for understanding ideas, however, concepts must always be understood as signs toward the Divine, rather than as definitive, absolute truths. This is the idea behind the statements of various Ancient Egyptian hymns:

> "No man has been able to seek out GOD's likeness. Though GOD can be seen in form and observation of GOD can be made at GOD's appearance, GOD cannot be understood... GOD cannot be seen with mortal eyes..."

These statements signify that no one who looks for God with the understanding of the ego-concept will be able to see God. What they will see is the world of time and space and deities created out of the imagination because they are looking through the impure intellect, mind and senses. In order to understand God one must transcend the human ego and thus become like God: transpersonal. It is only then that the correct understanding will dawn. The same idea is more explicitly stated in the Hindu *Upanishads* and the Taoist *Tao Te Ching*:

> "He truly knows Brahman who knows him as beyond knowledge; he who thinks that he knows, knows not. The ignorant think

that Brahman is known, but the wise know him to be beyond knowledge."

Kena Upanishad

"The Tao that can be told is not the eternal Tao.
The name that can be named is not the eternal name.
The nameless is the beginning of heaven and earth."

Tao Te Ching

When God is personified and given a specific name it is like trying to circumscribe the unconscious mind. Is there a limit in the unconscious mind? Is there a clear identity to the farthest reaches of your unconscious? No, therefore it cannot be circumscribed with any term or description. The concepts should only serve as temporary crutches for the mind to assist it in understanding the transcendental nature of the Divine until it is ready to grasp infinity and non-duality. Concepts should never be held onto because any and all concepts are faulty because the human mind is limited. Therefore, any attempt to classify God or circumscribe God with any description, location, name or form will be erroneous and idolatrous.

God cannot be defined in terms of time and space because God transcends these. In reality, the word "God" is a metaphor for that which transcends all human categories of thought and all mental concepts. The word "God" and the disciplines of religion and yoga philosophy are supposed to be a vehicle to get you in touch with the depths of your own being, but if you hold onto them as absolute realities you will miss the point which is being conveyed through the metaphors.

This way of holding onto the idea of God as a male personality or as a savior figure represents an erroneous understanding of religious symbolism and it is a source of strife among the world religions and of the relations between men and women. However, when you are able to transcend your own mind through the practices of yoga, then you are able to commune with that which is real, that which is non-dual, perfect and supremely "FULL".

The Significance of the Number Nine

There is important mystical significance related to the number nine (9) within Ancient Egyptian mystical philosophy. As introduced earlier, the Company of gods and goddesses of Ptah (Nun, Nunet, Huh, Huhet, Kuk, Kuket, Amon, Amonet) total eight in number and with Ptah they add up to nine. In the Company of gods and goddesses of Ra (Ra-Tem, Shu, Tefnut, Geb, Nut, Set, Osiris, Isis, Nephthys, and Horus) there is also a total of nine. The number nine is to be found in the very heart of Ancient Egyptian Mythology, the Cosmogony and Cosmogony itself, because the number nine is the basis of creation. This is why the number nine recurs in nature, in chemical and physics experiments.

Eight signifies the transient world of time and space and One is the number which symbolizes oneness, wholeness, All sight, All knowing, the Supreme Being, The Absolute. When the multiples of number eight (16, 24, and so on) are added up the total of their component numbers is less than eight (ex. 1+6=7). So while these numbers seem to be of greater value in reality they are of lesser value.

The world is like a dream that arises during sleep. The dream seems to be very real and abiding ("full") but when you wake up you discover that it is of lesser value than what you believed previously. The dream was an emanation from you and it has no reality unless you dream it. The dream is the eight and you are the one. You are the "fullness" which gives rise to your dream.

When the multiples of the number nine are added they all add up to 9. Thus, nine is the highest number. So when you discover *The Hidden Properties of Matter: Shetau Akhet* you are in reality discovering the essence of Creation and the Self (God). Creation is given value due to the presence of the Self who is the Absolute Reality which sustains Creation. Having discovered Shetau Akhet and your Higher Self as being one and the same, you have discovered all that there is to be known, you have achieved the number nine.

Finally, we will close this volume with an Ancient Egyptian quotation where God speaks of the works of creation and explains how all of the objects in creation are in reality emanations from him/herself:

Nebertcher, speaks: "I have done my will in everything on this earth. I have spread myself abroad therein, and I have made strong my hand. I was one by myself, for they [the gods and goddesses] had not been brought forth, and I had emitted from myself neither *Shu nor Tefnut*. I brought my own name into my mouth as a word of power, and I forthwith came into being under the form of things which are and as the Divine *Khepera*. I came into being from out of primeval matter, and from the beginning *I appeared as the form of the multitudinous things which exist; nothing whatsoever existed* at that time in this earth, and it was I who made whatsoever was made..

THE MYSTERIES OF SEKHMET

In order to more fully understand the teachings of Memphite Theology it is necessary to explore the female aspect of the Divine. The goddess Sekhmet is the consort of Ptah and the mystical wisdom behind this union will become clear when the name of the goddess is understood in more detail. Before we discover the hidden meanings of her name we need to go back in time first because the origins of the goddess are in the Theology of the city of Anu which emphasized the Company of gods and goddesses headed by Ra. In that theology Ra had nine children and these comprised the neters of Creation just as in Memphite theology Ptah had eight children. However, though the theologies came from different cities in reality they are related and are speaking of the same teaching with respect to the Supreme Being. One of Ra's daughter was Tefnut.

Tefnut represents moisture, such as when it rains. Rain allows plants to grow and it brings water for people to live. Tefnut is the powerful strength which is in the ocean of creation and she is the source of vitality for all living things. Tefnut is commonly referred to as moisture but she is much more than that. Her iconography, which includes the lioness, the serpent on the crown of the head, the papyrus scepter and the ankh holds important mystical symbolism. These icons symbolize the power of nature (lioness), life (ankh), the papyrus scepter symbolizes among other things the power of knowledge. The serpent symbolizes the power of the Life Force energy which courses through nature and which sustains all life. When it is placed on the crown of the head it signifies that the power has

161

reached full expression. It is related to the discipline known as Serpent Power Yoga or the cultivation of the internal Life Force energy. When this discipline is taken to completion a human being can develop his or her individual Life Force and then join it with the Universal Life Force (God) and thereby attain spiritual enlightenment. This is a process which occurs naturally in all human beings as they experience life and reincarnation. However, when yoga is practiced the process of spiritual evolution is enhanced and accelerated.*

Since Ptah symbolizes the Supreme Being in Memphite Theology who creates the world through the power of his thoughts the relationship between he and Sekhmet becomes clear. The name Sekhmet arises from the root sekhem which means Life Force and power. Thus, Sekhmet is the cosmic force which Ptah emanates and through which he works out the manifestation of the universe. Thus, Ptah is the cause while Sekhmet is the dynamic aspect of the Divine.

Worshiping the goddess means working with the power of creation and the cultivation of the Serpent Power as well as the discipline of mind control. This process can be carried out through the study of the teachings related to Memphite Theology and meditation on the mind of Ptah by seeing oneself as the immovable spirit who is operating through the animal life force. The lioness is also the symbol of power for the goddess in India. The goddess Durga of India is the consort of Shiva, who is part of the Hindu Trinity *Brahma-Vishnu-Shiva* in much the same way as Ptah is part of the Ancient Egyptian Trinity Amun-Ra-Ptah. Durga rides on a lion and her worship, like that of Sekhmet, bestows the power to overcome obstacles on the spiritual path.

The goddess Sekhmet may be worshipped in her dual aspect as Sekhemti. In this aspect she is also referred to as Uadjit and Nekhebet, Aset and Nebthet, Maati, etc. Therefore, the wisdom of the double goddess with respect to manifestation of the life force is the science of unraveling the duality of life which leads to the discovery of the oneness behind all creation.

*See the book *The Serpent Power: The Development of the Internal Life Force*.

May you discover all of the
Hidden Properties of Matter

TEFNUT -
The Power of Water

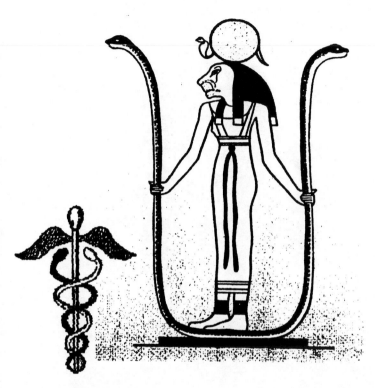

Above: The goddess Sekhmet is holding the two forces (positive and negative) which together manifest as the opposites of creation. So in this aspect Sekhmet is likened to the caduceus of Tehuti. Sekhmet is the central channel while the two serpents symbolize the solar and lunar. Note that the two serpents are in reality one serpent with two heads. This signifies that the energy, while appearing as opposites in the form of two serpents (positive and negative), is in reality two aspects of the same energy. When the opposite forces in the mind and body are harmonized there is a dawning of the vision of universality and union which underlies all.

Sekhmet is closely related to the serpent goddess in all her forms of manifestation and therefore she is also a presiding deity of the Serpent Power or internal Life Force energy.

The Goddess
Durga
of India

Questions for Reflection and Study

The following questions and exercises are designed for those taking the Egyptian Yoga course and are based on this volume and on Egyptian Yoga: The Philosophy of Enlightenment. However, anyone who works through them will gain a deeper insight into the themes expressed in this book.

1- What were the forms of energy originally studied in the scientific discipline of Physics (classical physics)?

_____

_____

_____

_____

_____

_____

_____

2- Which system replaced classical physics and why?

_____

_____

_____

_____

_____

_____

_____

3- When did relativity theory come into physics?

_____

_____

_____

_____

_____

_____

4- What has caused a major revolution in the scientific community?

_____

_____

_____

_____

_____

_____

5- What is the most important discovery of modern physics?

_____

_____

_____

_____

_____

_____

_____

6- How is this discovery related to ancient mystical philosophy?

_____

_____   _____

_____

_____

_____

_____

_____

7- What did ancient mystical philosophers know about the human mind and senses?

_____

_____

_____

_____

_____

_____

_____

8- What have the Sages of ancient times compared the ordinary state of human existence to?

_____

_____

_____

_____

_____

_____

_____

9- What were the Ancient Egyptian Sages saying in the Ancient Egyptian Pyramid Texts 8000 years ago?

_____

_____

_____

_____

_____

_____

10- What did ancient yogis discover about the universe long ago?

_____

_____

_____

_____

_____

_____

_____

11- What is Memphite Theology?

_____

_____

_____

_____

_____

_____

12- What is the Ancient Egyptian Trinity and how does it relate to Memphite Theology?

_____

_____

_____

_____

_____

_____

13- What must you do with the information in this volume at this level of teaching?

_____

_____

_____

_____

_____

_____

14- Who is the main character in Memphite Theology?

_____

_____

_____

_____

_____

_____

15- What does this character represent?

_____

_____

_____

_____

_____

_____

16- What is the full name of the Ancient Egyptian Trinity?

_____

_____

_____

_____

_____

_____

_____

17- Did God create the universe by magic?

_____

_____

_____

_____

_____

_____

_____

18- What is the underlying essence of the universe? Explain.

_____

_____

_____

_____

_____

_____

_____

19- What are *neters*?

_____

_____

_____

_____

_____

_____

20- Is the information gathered by the human mind and senses reliable? Explain.

_____

_____

_____

_____

_____

21- For what purpose have the ancient sages developed the disciplines of yoga?

_____

_____

_____

_____

_____

_____

_____

22- What is the difference between knowing something intellectually and knowing it intuitionally?

_____

_____

_____

_____

_____

_____

23- What is Nun? (use a separate sheet if necessary)

_____

_____

_____

_____

_____

23b- Explain the order-level of Subtly in all existence?

_____

_____

_____

_____

_____

_____

_____

23c- Why are physical bodies (including the human body) alive and why are they dead?

_____

_____

_____

_____

_____

_____

_____

23d- What is cosmic will and what is the will of an un-enlightened person?

_____

_____

_____

_____

_____

_____

_____

24- What is matter?

_____

_____

_____

_____

_____

_____

25- Explain how matter vibrates and how this affects the way matter appears.

_____

_____

_____

_____

25- What is an Atom?

_____

_____

_____

_____

_____

_____

26- What are molecules?

_____
_____
_____
_____
_____
_____
_____

27- What are "Physical Objects"?

_____
_____
_____
_____
_____
_____

28- According to scientific evidence, what composes all matter?

_____
_____
_____
_____
_____
_____

29- What is a particle accelerator?

_____

_____

_____

_____

_____

_____

30- What does the formula $E=MC^2$ represent?

_____

_____

_____

_____

_____

31- What happens every time you breath out?

_____

_____

_____

_____

_____

_____

32- What are Sekhem and Prana, and Chi?

_____

_____

_____

_____

_____

_____

_____

33- What is "Dark Matter"?

_____

_____

_____

_____

_____

_____

34- Explain how a particle accelerator works and what particle accelerator experiments have shown about matter?

_____

_____

_____

_____

_____

35- Is "reality", the world a constant and abiding factor? Explain.

_____

_____

_____

_____

_____

_____

_____

36- What is space?

_____

_____

_____

_____

37- In reality, time does not exist. What most people call time is in reality an attempt to explain the process by which matter changes. Therefore, the grosser the form of matter, the slower the rate of change. For this reason a spirit, which is subtler, may remain in the disembodied state for a moment while the passage of time on earth may seem to be a millennia. Read the story of *Mer-ka-re* and explain how it relates to the theory of relativity of Einstein.

_____

_____

_____

_____

_____

_____

_____

Assignment- 1: Exercise and One page essay.

Choose a quiet time, perhaps after your meditation time and reflect on the teaching of Memphite Theology and imagine yourself as the creator and sustainer of the universe. Imagine yourself having the thought first and then manifesting that thought through the organs of action and also imagine yourself bringing objects into existence by merely thinking about them. This is what occurs in your dreams without your control. Now through your mind you will perform the same actions while in the waking state under your control. See yourself as the source of all thoughts and the vivifier of all objects. See yourself as being the cause which supports all of the objects of your mind's creation. Watch all of these as your projection, which you can withdraw back into yourself at any moment. Be separate and detached from these projections. See them as transitory creations.

Write down your experiences in your spiritual journal.

Other Books From C. M. Books
P.O.Box 570459
Miami, Florida, 33257
(305) 378-6253 Fax: (305) 378-6253

This book is part of a series on the study and practice of Ancient Egyptian Yoga and Mystical Spirituality based on the writings of Dr. Muata Abhaya Ashby. They are also part of the Egyptian Yoga Course provided by the Sema Institute of Yoga. Below you will find a listing of the other books in this series. For more information send for the Egyptian Yoga Book-Audio-Video Catalog or the Egyptian Yoga Course Catalog.

Now you can study the teachings of Egyptian and Indian Yoga wisdom and Spirituality with the Egyptian Yoga Mystical Spirituality Series. The Egyptian Yoga Series takes you through the Initiation process and lead you to understand the mysteries of the soul and the Divine and to attain the highest goal of life: ENLIGHT-ENMENT. The *Egyptian Yoga Series*, takes you on an in depth study of Ancient Egyptian mythology and their inner mystical meaning. Each Book is prepared for the serious student of the mystical sciences and provides a study of the teachings along with exercises, assignments and projects to make the teachings understood and effective in real life. The Series is part of the Egyptian Yoga course but may be purchased even if you are not taking the course. The series is ideal for study groups.
Prices subject to change.

The Egyptian Yoga Book Series

**EGYPTIAN YOGA:
THE PHILOSOPHY OF
ENLIGHTENMENT**
ISBN 1-884564-01-1

**INITIATION INTO
EGYPTIAN YOGA**
Teacher-Disciple, Daily Practice
ISBN 1-884564-02-X

**THE
AUSARIAN RESURRECTION**
The Ancient Egyptian Bible
ISBN 1-884564-27-5 Soft Cover

**THE
CYCLES OF TIME**
The History of Yoga In Egypt
ISBN 1-884564-13-5

**MYSTICISM OF
USHET REKHAT**
Worship of the Divine Mother
ISBN 1-884564-18-6

**THE HIDDEN
PROPERTIES OF MATTER**
The Mystical Nature of Creation
ISBN 1-884564-07-0

The Egyptian Yoga Book Series

**EGYPTIAN YOGA
EXERCISE WORKOUT BOOK**
Movement of the Gods and Goddesses
ISBN 1-884564-00-3

MEDITATION
The Ancient Egyptian
Path to Enlightenment
ISBN 1-884564-27-7

**THE MYSTICAL TEACHINGS OF
THE AUSARIAN RESURRECTION**
The Third Level of the Mysteries
ISBN 1-884564-22-4

THE HYMNS OF AMUN
Theban Theology and
Mystical Psychology
320 pages 5.5"x 8.5"

**HEALING THE
CRIMINAL HEART**
Redeption through
Righteous Living
40 pages   5.5"x 8.5"

THE SERPENT POWER
Mystical teachings of the
Inner Life Force
204 pages 5.5"x 8.5"

The Egyptian Yoga Book Series

**GOD IN THE UNIVERSE
GOD IN THE HEART**
The Oneness of the Self in
Creation and the Soul
ISBN 1-884564-24-0

**THE BLOOMING LOTUS
OF DIVINE LOVE**
The Spiritual Path of Cosmic Love
ISBN 1-884564-11-9

EGYPTIAN PROVERBS
The Foundations of
Maat Philosophy
ISBN 1-884564-00-3

**EGYPTIAN
TANTRA YOGA**
Sex Sublimation and
Universal Consciousness
203 pages 5.5"x 8.5"

**THE WISDOM OF
MAATI**
Righteousness and
Spiritual Enlightenment
222 pages 5.5"x 8.5"

The Egyptian Yoga Book Series

THE STORY OF
ASAR, ASET and HERU
Children's Storybook/Coloring book
41 pages 8.5"X 11"
ISBN: 1-884564-31-3 $9.99

The Parents Guide To
The Ausarian Resurrection Myth:
64 pages 5.5"x 8.5"
ISBN: 1-884564-30-5 $5.99

The Sema Institute of Yoga - Cruzian Mystic Books
To order send check or money order plus $3.50 for postage
for the first item and $1 for each additional item to:
P.O. Box 570459, Miami Fla. 33257
(305) 378-6253

EGYPTIAN YOGA:
THE PHILOSOPHY OF ENLIGHTENMENT
by
Dr. Muata Abhaya Ashby

An original, fully illustrated work, including hieroglyphs, detailing the meaning of the Egyptian mysteries, tantric yoga, psycho-spiritual and physical exercises. Egyptian Yoga is a guide to the practice of the highest spiritual philosophy which leads to absolute freedom from human misery and to immortality. It is well known by scholars that Egyptian philosophy is the basis of Western and Middle Eastern religious philosophies such as *Christianity, Islam, Judaism,* the *Kabbalah,* and Greek philosophy, but what about Indian philosophy, Yoga and Taoism? What were the original teachings? How can they be practiced today? What is the source of pain and suffering in the world and what is the solution? Discover the deepest mysteries of the mind and universe within and outside of your self.
216 Pages 8.5" X 11" ISBN: 1-884564-01-1 Soft $17.95 U.S.

THE AUSARIAN RESURRECTION:
The Ancient Egyptian Bible
by
Dr. Muata Abhaya Ashby

The Ancient Sages created stories based on human and superhuman beings whose struggles, aspirations, needs and desires ultimately lead them to discover their true Self. The myth of Isis, Osiris and Horus is no exception in this area. While there is no one source where the entire story may be found, pieces of it are inscribed in various ancient temples walls, tombs, steles and papyri. For the first time available, the complete myth of Osiris, Isis and Horus has been compiled from original Ancient Egyptian, Greek and Coptic Texts. This epic myth has been richly illustrated with reliefs from the temple of Horus at Edfu, the temple of Isis at Philae, the temple of Osiris at Abydos, the temple of Hathor at Denderah and various papyri, inscriptions and reliefs.

Discover the myth which inspired the teachings of the *Shetaut Neter* (Egyptian Mystery System - Egyptian Yoga) and the

Egyptian Book of Coming Forth By Day. Also, discover the three levels of Ancient Egyptian Religion, how to understand the mysteries of the Tuat or Astral World and how to discover the abode of the Supreme in the Amenta, *The Other World.*

The ancient religion of Osiris, Isis and Horus, if properly understood, contains all of the elements necessary to lead the sincere aspirant to attain immortality through inner self-discovery. This volume presents the entire myth and explores the main mystical themes and rituals associated with the myth for understating human existence, creation and the way to achieve spiritual emancipation - *Resurrection.* The Osirian myth is so powerful that it influenced and is still having an effect on the major world religions. Discover the origins and mystical meaning of the Christian Trinity, the Eucharist ritual and the ancient origin of the birthday of Jesus Christ.

191 Pages 8.5" X 11" Hard Cover ISBN: 1-884564-12-7 $29.99 U.S. Soft Cover ISBN: 1-884564-27-5 $17.95

INITIATION INTO EGYPTIAN YOGA:
The Secrets of Sheti
by
Dr. Muata Abhaya Ashby

Sheti: Spiritual discipline or program, to go deeply into the mysteries, to study the mystery teachings and literature profoundly, to penetrate the mysteries.

♀ You will learn about the mysteries of initiation into the teachings and practice of Yoga and how to become an Initiate of the mystical sciences.

This insightful manual is the first in a series which introduces you to the goals of daily spiritual and yoga practices: Meditation, Diet, Words of Power and the ancient wisdom teachings.

150 pages 8.5" X 11" ISBN 1-884564-02-X Soft Cover $15.99 U.S.

MYSTICISM OF USHET REKHAT:
Worship of the Divine Mother

The Supreme Being may be worshipped as father or as mother. *Ushet Rekhat* or *Mother Worship*, is the spiritual process of worshipping the Divine in the form of the Divine Goddess. It celebrates the most important forms of the Goddess including *Nathor, Maat, Aset, Arat, Amentet and Hathor* and explores their mystical meaning as well as the rising of *Sirius*, the star of Aset (Isis) and the new birth of Hor (Horus). The end of the year is a time of reckoning, reflection and engendering a new or renewed positive movement toward attaining spiritual enlightenment. The Mother Worship devotional meditation ritual, performed on five days during the month of December and on New Year's Eve, is based on the Ushet Rekhit. During the ceremony, the cosmic forces, symbolized by Sirius ✯ and the constellation of Orion ✯✯✯, are harnessed through the understanding and devotional attitude of the participant. This propitiation draws the light of wisdom and health to all those who share in the ritual, leading to prosperity and wisdom.
$5.99 - 64 pages. 5.5"x 8.5"   ISBN 1-884564-18-6

EGYPTIAN PROVERBS:
TEMT TCHAAS

Temt Tchaas means: collection of Ancient Egyptian Proverbs
  ⚲ How to live according to MAAT Philosophy.
  ⚲ Beginning Meditation.
  ⚲ All proverbs are indexed for easy searches.
For the first time in one volume, Ancient Egyptian proverbs, wisdom teachings and meditations, fully illustrated with hieroglyphic text and symbols. EGYPTIAN PROVERBS is a unique collection of knowledge and wisdom which you can put into practice today and transform your life. **160 pages. 5.5"x 8.5" $9.95 U.S ISBN: 1-884564-00-3**

EGYPTIAN YOGA EXERCISE
WORKOUT BOOK
Thef Neteru:
The Movement of The Gods and Goddesses

Discover the physical postures and exercises practiced thousands of years ago in Ancient Egypt which are today known as Yoga exercises. This work is based on the pictures and teachings from the Creation story of Ra, The Osirian Resurrection Myth and the carvings and reliefs from various Temples in Ancient Egypt. **100 Pages 8.5" X 11" ISBN 1-884564-10-0 Soft Cover $16.99 Exercise video $16.99**
Available late Fall 1997.

THE CYCLES OF TIME:
The Ancient Origins of Yoga in Egypt and India

This Volume will cover the ancient origins of Yoga and establish a link between the cultures of Ancient Egypt and ancient and modern India. This Volume is of paramount importance because it shows that Egyptian Philosophy began over 30,000 years ago and did not die out along with Egyptian society but that it was carried on by the Sages and Saints who left Egypt at the time of its social collapse. **200 pages. 5.5"x 8.5" ISBN 1-884564-13-5 $14.99**

THE ` PROPERTIES OF MATTER:
Egyptian Physics and
Yoga Metaphysics.

This Volume will go deeper into the philosophy of God as creation and will explore the concepts of modern science and how they correlate with ancient teachings. This Volume will lay the ground work for the understanding of the philosophy of universal consciousness and the initiatic/yogic insight into who or what is God? **178 pages. 5.5"x 8.5" ISBN 1-884564-07-0 $14.99**

GOD IN THE UNIVERSE, GOD IN THE HEART
Who is God in the light of
Yoga Philosophy?

Through the study of ancient myth and the illumination of initiatic understanding the idea of God is expanded from the mythological comprehension to the metaphysical. Then this metaphysical understanding is related to you, the student, so as to begin understanding your true divine nature. **156 pages 5.5"x 8.5" ISBN 1-884564-24-0 $12.99**

THE MYSTICAL TEACHINGS
OF
THE AUSARIAN RESURRECTION

This Volume will detail the myth of the Osirian Resurrection and The Story of Horus and Set and their mystical implications in the life of the aspirant/initiate. Then this volume will turn to a line by line mystical reading of the myth in order to uncover the mystical implications of the epic story. Mythology will come alive as a message from the Sages of ancient times to the initiates and not just as stories for entertainment. This Volume is special because it links the individual student to the myth and thereby gives her/him deep insight into his/her own true nature and how to practice the religion of Osiris, Isis and Horus. This volume may be used as a companion to the book *The Ausarian Resurrection: The Ancient Egyptian Bible* by Muata Ashby (see the description above). **232 pages 5.5"x 8.5" ISBN: 1-884564-22-4 $14.99**

THE WISDOM OF MAATI:
Spiritual Enlightenment Through the Path of Virtue

Known as Karma Yoga in India, the teachings of MAAT for living virtuously and with orderly wisdom are explained and the student is to begin practicing the precepts of Maat in daily life so as to promote the process of purification of the heart in preparation for the judgment of the soul. This judgment will be understood not as an event that will occur at the time of death but as an event that occurs continuously, at every moment in the life of the individual. The student will learn how to become allied with the forces of the Higher Self and to thereby begin cleansing the mind (heart) of impurities so as to attain a higher vision of reality. 210 **pages 5.5"x 8.5" ISBN 1-884564-20-8 $14.99**

EGYPTIAN TANTRA YOGA:
The Art of Sex Sublimation and Universal Consciousness

This Volume will expand on the male and female principles within the human body and in the universe and further detail the sublimation of sexual energy into spiritual energy. The student will study the deities Min and Hathor, Osiris and Isis, Geb and Nut and discover the mystical implications for a practical spiritual discipline. This Volume will also focus on the Tantric aspects of Ancient Egyptian and Indian mysticism, the purpose of sex and the mystical teachings of sexual sublimation which lead to self-knowledge and enlightenment. **203 pages 5.5"x 8.5" ISBN 1-884564-03-8 $14.99**

THE BLOOMING LOTUS OF DIVINE LOVE
The Process of
Mystical Transformation and
The Path of Divine Love

This Volume will focus on the ancient wisdom teachings and how to use them in a scientific process for self-transformation. Also, this volume will detail the process of transformation from ordinary consciousness to cosmic consciousness through the integrated practice of the teachings and the path of Devotional Love toward the Divine. **225 pages 5.5"x 8.5" ISBN 1-884564-11-9 $14.99**

MEDITATION
The Ancient Egyptian Path to Enlightenment

Many people do not know about the rich history of meditation practice in Ancient Egypt. This volume outlines the theory of meditation and presents the Ancient Egyptian Hieroglyphic text which give instruction as to the nature of the mind and its three modes of expression. It also presents the texts which give instruction on the practice of meditation for spiritual enlightenment and unity with the Divine. This volume allows the reader to begin practicing meditation by explaining, in easy to understand terms, the simplest form of meditation and working up to the most advanced form which was practiced in ancient times and which is still practiced by yogis around the world in modern times. **268 pages 5.5"x 8.5" ISBN 1-884564-27-7 $14.99**

HEALING THE CRIMINAL HEART
Introduction to Maat Philosophy, Yoga and Spiritual Redemption Through the Path of Virtue

Who is a criminal? Is there such a thing as a criminal heart? What is the source of evil and sinfulness and is there any way to rise above it? Is there redemption for those who have committed sins, even the worst crimes?

Ancient Egyptian mystical psychology holds important answers to these questions. Over ten thousand years ago mystical psychologists, the Sages of Ancient Egypt, studied and charted the human mind and spirit and laid out a path which will lead to spiritual redemption, prosperity and enlightenment.

This introductory volume brings forth the teachings of the Ausarian Resurrection, the most important myth of Ancient Egypt, with relation to the faults of human existence: anger, hatred, greed, lust, animosity, discontent, ignorance, egoism jealousy, bitterness, and a myriad of psycho-spiritual ailments which keep a human being in a state of negativity and adversity. **40 pages 5.5"x 8.5" ISBN: 1-884564-17-8 $3.99**

THE HYMNS OF AMUN
The Mystical Wisdom of Ancient Egyptian Theban Theology

Take a fascinating journey back in time and discover the teachings which constituted the epitome of Ancient Egyptian spiritual wisdom. The teachings of the city of Thebes were the crowning achievement of the Sages and Saints of Ancient Egypt because they summarize and comprehensively explain the mysteries of the entire symbolism of the Ancient Egyptian pantheon of gods and goddesses that emanate from a Supreme Being who forms Creation while emerging as a Trinity. Theban Theology sheds light on the Trinity system of Christianity as well as that of Hinduism in India and establishes the standard mystical keys for understanding the profound mystical symbolism of the Triad of Human consciousness which leads to spiritual enlightenment. This volume introduces the teachings of Ancient Egypt through the religious hymns of Amun. **311 pages 5.5"x 8.5"   ISBN: 1-884564-08-9 $15.99**

THE SERPENT POWER:
The Ancient Egyptian Mystical Wisdom
of the Inner Life Force.

This Volume specifically deals with the latent life Force energy of the universe and in the human body, its control and sublimation. How to develop the Life Force energy of the subtle body. This Volume will introduce the esoteric wisdom of the science of how virtuous living acts in a subtle and mysterious way to cleanse the latent psychic energy conduits and vortices of the spiritual body. **204 pages 5.5"x 8.5"   ISBN 1-884564-19-4 $14.99**

The Parents Guide To The Ausarian Resurrection Myth:
How to Teach Yourself and Your Child
the Principles of Universal Mystical Religion.

This insightful manual brings for the timeless wisdom of the ancient through the Ancient Egyptian myth of Asar, Aset and

Heru and the mystical teachings contained in it for parents who want to guide their children to understand and practice the teachings of mystical spirituality. This manual may be used with the children's storybook *The Story of Asar, Aset and Heru* by Dr. Muata Abhaya Ashby. **64 pages** **5.5"x 8.5"** **ISBN: 1-884564-30-5** **$5.99**

The Story of Asar, Aset and Heru:
An Ancient Egyptian Legend

Now for the first time, the most ancient myth of Ancient Egypt comes alive for children. Inspired by the books *The Ausarian Resurrection: The Ancient Egyptian Bible* and *The Mystical Teachings of The Ausarian Resurrection*, **The Story of Asar, Aset and Heru** is an easy to understand and thrilling tale which inspired the children of Ancient Egypt to aspire to greatness and righteousness.

If you and your child have enjoyed stories like *The Lion King* and *Star Wars you will love **The Story of Asar, Aset and Heru**.* Also, if you know the story of Jesus and Krishna you will discover than Ancient Egypt had a similar myth and that this myth carries important spiritual teachings for living a fruitful and fulfilling life.

This book may be used along with *The Parents Guide To The Ausarian Resurrection Myth: How to Teach Yourself and Your Child the Principles of Universal Mystical Religion.* The guide provides some background to the Ausarian Resurrection myth and it also gives insight into the mystical teachings contained in it which you may introduce to your child. It is designed for parents who wish to grow spiritually with their children and it serves as an introduction for those who would like to study the Ausarian Resurrection Myth in depth and to practice its teachings. **41 pages** **8.5" X 11"** **ISBN: 1-884564-31-3** **$10.99**

Egyptian Yoga Audio Cassette Series

Introduction to Egyptian Yoga Tape I $9.99, Tape II $9.99 Three hours
Maat Workshop I How to Practice the Teachings Tape I $9.99, Tape II $9.99 Three hours
The Serpent Power I Music and Meditation Tape I $9.99, Tape II $9.99 Three hours
Ushet I: Daily worship and Meditation $9.99   30 Minutes each side
Indus Kamit Kush - Yoga in Ancient Egypt and India $14.99   Two hours
The Egyptian Yoga Exercise Workout $9.99   One hour
The Inner Meaning of The Egyptian, Christian and Indian Trinity $14.99 -
Initiation Into Egyptian Yoga - $19.99 Two tapes
The Initiatic Way of Education - $14.99 Two hours
The Meditation and Chanting Workshop Series - Four Tapes 3 hours-40 minutes $30.00

Egyptian Yoga Video Cassette Series

Introduction to Egyptian Yoga $19.99
Indus - Kamit - Kush Yoga in Ancient Egypt and India $19.99
Thef Neteru: The Movement of The Gods and Goddesses, The Egyptian Yoga Exercise Workout $19.99
The Inner Meaning of The Egyptian, Christian and Indian Trinity $19.99
Meditation and Chanting Workshop 3 hours-40 minutes $40.00
Initiation Into Egyptian Yoga Video with manual - Class 1 of the the Course in Yoga and Mystical Spirituality at Florida International University in Miami Florida $24.99

Copyright 1996-1997 **Dr. Reginald Muata Abhaya Ashby**
Sema Institute of Yoga
P.O.Box 570459
Miami, Florida, 33257
(305) 378-6253 Fax: (305) 378-6253